Whoopi

Likes Her Bacon Crispy

65 Fascinating Excerpts from the Memoirs of Famous and Infamous Women

Compiled by J. Ajlouny

Whoopi

Likes Her Bacon Crispy

65 Fascinating Excerpts
from the Memoirs of
Famous and Infamous Women

Compiled by J. Ajlouny

PUSH PULL PRESS

Fresh Ink Group
Guntersville

Whoopi Likes Her Bacon Crispy
65 Fascinating Excerpts from the Memoirs of Famous and Infamous Women

Copyright © 2021
by J. Ajlouny
All rights reserved

Push Pull Press
An Imprint of:
The Fresh Ink Group, LLC
1021 Blount Avenue, #931
Guntersville, AL 35976
Email: info@FreshInkGroup.com
FreshInkGroup.com

Edition 1.0   2021

Caricature Artwork by Duy Phan / FIG
Cover design by Stephen Geez / FIG
Book design by Amit Dey / FIG
Associate publisher Lauren A. Smith / FIG

Cataloging-in-Publication Recommendations:
BIO013000 BIOGRAPHY & AUTOBIOGRAPHY / Rich & Famous
BIO022000 BIOGRAPHY& AUTOBIOGRAPHY / Women
PER019000 PERFORMING ARTS / Storytelling

Library of Congress Control Number: 2021919887

ISBN-13: 978-1-947867-44-4 Papercover
ISBN-13: 978-1-947867-45-1 Hardcover
ISBN-13: 978-1-947867-46-8 Ebooks

Table of Contents

Introduction

I had a revelation one day while I was reading Lauren Bacall's first memoir, which was published in 1965. This is fascinating stuff, I thought, even though I really didn't have much personal interest in her or her career. The stories she tells are quite interesting. They are informative, elucidating, and entertaining. I like the Golden Era of Hollywood as much as anybody, but I was never curious enough to read about it. I like Humphrey Bogart, too, but I'm not particularly interested in the tales his widow tells about him, though some of them are indeed interesting. But the more I read, the more curious I became. By the end, I quite enjoyed her autobiography. I then learned that some thirty years later she wrote a second memoir, so I read that one, too. It covers some of the same territory, but adds the second half of her life and career to the story. I then moved on to the autobiographies of Ava Gardner and Shelley Winters. Then I found many more in my local library, including those of Shirley Temple, Katharine Hepburn, Eartha Kitt, Joan Rivers, Cybill Shepherd, and my favorite bombshell, Raquel Welch. And I enjoyed reading each one. And then I found I couldn't stop searching for and reading the memoirs of famous women. I quickly moved on from movie and television stars to the world of politics, athletics, and entertainment. Pretty soon I had fifty and then or sixty books under my proverbial belt. It's great work if you can get it.

Then it hit me: These stories are ripe for telling orally. They are incisive, funny, poignant, and easy to listen to. Of course, when the listener is familiar with the teller, it makes the story all the more appealing. So, I decided to collect excerpts from these books and string them together for presentation from a stage—to make a theater piece out of them. A good part of my previous career was developing and promoting stage shows that raise funds for theatre companies and theatre programs. This idea fit the bill, and it was a lot more pleasurable to create.

The list of women represented here is only a function of which books were readily available within the time frame I was working. Many I had absolutely no interest in but read because I figured somewhere in here there has got to be a good little story that people will enjoy listening too. And I was correct. Well, there is one exception which shall remain nameless. The author is a very famous woman—an Oscar winner still very much with us. I read her book but could not find a single sentence that I liked or thought would work within the context of the whole. I was in disbelief. So, I read it again, two months later. Still nothing. So, I did something I found hard to do, I set it aside and said, "Oh well, not every woman is entitled to enter this house."

Every one of these excerpts has something to offer everybody. I promise the reader and the listener that this is true. Not one of these stories is a bore. Quite the contrary, they are clever, surprising, and witty. My goal was to replicate what the best short-story writers try to do as their tales unfold one by one. I purposely kept them fair-use brief, as brevity is the soul of wit, as Polonius opined to Prince Hamel in Hamlet. I searched for the nuggets, and I believe I found them.

Notes for Stage Performance

*T*his collection of excerpts was initially conceived as a live stage presentation. It is an example of what has been termed Reader's Theatre and modeled after this genre's leading example, Eve Ensler's *The Vagina Monologues*. Ensler's play, which is a consolidation of interviews read from the stage by a cohort of three to five actors, did something I do not even attempt to emulate. It raised awareness of women's rights and the sanctity of women's bodies. To that end, the show migrated around the globe and accomplished two important goals, apart from offering an entertaining and thought-provoking mix of stories about a taboo topic. First, it galvanized women's groups to assert themselves and thus jump-start a movement which has evolved into such manifestations as #MeToo and #TimesUp, among others. Second, it created a community-scope event that brought people together, first as audiences, but eventually as individuals supporting the needs of their local women's rights groups, and in doing so, amplified a collective voice of aspiration.

I recall attending two shows of this genre in the early 2000s. The first was titled The *Marijuana-logues*, mostly about the dumb things people do when they are high; and *My Very First Time*, a collection of stories about how people lost their virginity. Both were simple compilations of interview shows which sought only to entertain. No names or likenesses were used or even suggested. The anonymity such scripts offer is indeed enticing. I can't say that these shows were presented as fundraisers, but they could have been, and perhaps should have been. One element of this genre, not previously described, is the opportunity to invite local celebrities (wage-free of course) to be the readers. This adds to the attraction and localizes the presentation. *Whoopi Likes Her Bacon Crispy* seeks to take advantage of this model, but with less gravitas. I've always believed theater should be both illuminating and entertaining, in equal measure if possible, and that's why I put this collection together.

The vision is simple: three or four readers on a bare stage. Each has a script in a three-ring binder with her excerpts highlighted. They can pick and choose which ones they wish to present. Then they read them in a sequence they deem suitable. The audience is intrigued. The audience is beguiled. The audience is entertained. They are happy they came. And they like your theatre company even more now. If you play it right, you have a new patron.

It is my sincere hope that the presentation of this compilation as a stage play will raise a lot of money for a lot of theatre companies and other non-profit organizations. And it is my hope that audiences will enjoy the show so much that they will forget they just dropped a wad for the privilege of attending. I hope you will enjoy listening or reading them as much as I did. I trust you will.

Madeleine Albright

Madeline Albright

Madame Secretary
By Madeline Albright
Miramax Books, 2003

My Own Plane

Not surprisingly, I discovered that the best thing about being Secretary of State was having my own plane. I remain grateful to the men and women of the U.S. Air Force who kept me safely aloft on more than one hundred foreign trips and one million miles over my four-year term. And to the head of my administrative staff, who made sure the thousand moving parts involved in every trip came together in the right way and the right time.

One of those parts was my luggage, which was always placed in my private cabin for security reasons. And because I often needed to make quick wardrobe changes depending on the temperatures of our destination. It was not uncommon for us to travel back and forth between the hottest and coldest climates and that was never easy or fun. Of course, almost all of my predecessors had wives to pack for them. I didn't, so I developed my own crazy routine. I would arrive home in Washington D.C. late with a schedule of events, sit down in front to the TV, and write down what I would need to wear for each engagement, even figuring out which pin would complement my outfit the best. Then the fun would begin as I had to remember where the clothes I had selected actually were. And if I could still fit into them since the last trip. Ambassadors have an opportunity to try an awful lot of wonderful food and I was no different. If anyone had appeared at my house at such a time, they would have discovered a very un-secretary of state-like person running around muttering to herself. At first I was good about keeping track of what I had worn in each country, so I wouldn't repeat, but after a while I gave that up as too difficult and unimportant.

Like many American women, I tried a variety of exercise and diet programs. When I was on the plane, the crew did its best to accommodate whatever regimen I was on. For example, they found room for a portable stair-stepper and weights and always had fresh tuna fish and the crackers I adored. But no matter what or where, however, during each trip I invariably experienced that special moment when exhaustion overcame discipline and my favorite taco salad smothered with everything arrived, along with smuggled in KitKat candy bars. I figured I deserved it but never enjoyed it without sold feelings of guilt.

Occasionally I would enjoy a movie while in the air but I made it a point to avoid international thrillers because they reminded me too much about the problems of my day job. I recall one exception, however, when I was invited to fly with President Clinton to a summit in Japan. It was terribly ironic but we watched Harrison Ford in the thriller *Air Force One* while on Air Force One. I didn't like it.

Julie Andrews

Julie Andrews

Home
By Julie Andrews
Hyperion, 2008

The Artifice of Modeling

In the summer of 1958, shortly after "My Fair Lady" opened at the Drury Lane Theater in London to smashing reviews, the producers were offered the very flattering invitation to have the main characters Henry Higgins, played by Rex Harrison and Eliza Doolittle, my role, added to the collection of Madame Tussaud's Wax Museum.

To accomplish this task, I had consultation with its designers and photos were taken of me modeling costumes and extensive measurements were taken of my entire body and face. Very early in the morning days afterward a gentleman came to my apartment with six long, leather bound jewel cases under his arm. It was very mysterious. He flung back the case lids with a flourish and revealed pair after pair of glass eyes, all different colors and staring in all different directions. I was startled. He proceeded to examine my eyes, and then selected eyeballs from his collection one at a time, comparing them to my own to find a match. He muttered to himself "No, not quite right" or "No not bloodshot enough," and "No not yellow enough." It was chilling and bizarre. Not long afterward, my manager

Charlie Tucker decided he wanted a portrait of me as Eliza for his office and he commissioned the famous painter Pectro Annigoni, who had done many portraits of members of the royal family. As I was to learn, much to my chagrin, Annigoni was an arrogant man, the epitome of the temperamental artist. He demanded total dedication and punctuality from me.

Accordingly photographs of me wearing Eliza's flower market girl costume were taken and posted around his studio while he worked. He also required several live sittings with me as well. Since I was performing in the show eight times per week, planning my wedding and having fittings for my gown and with everything else going on, my life was hectic and I had difficulty slotting everything in. And of course the inevitable happened. I arrived late at his studio one day. He was so miffed that he locked me out and left me all alone on the street. I could see the curtain twitching at his upstairs window as he peered down at my anger and discomfort. So, I knew he was home and I called to him to let him know I knew. But he would not relent. My manager had to plead with him to complete the portraits. Thankfully the results are worth the effort. The finished painting is wonderful, and he really captured the essence of Eliza. But what is noteworthy is not the portrait itself but the extraordinary coincidence that is the background he included a half-hidden poster with the words, "The Sound of…." This was almost ten years before *The Sound of Music* was ever written. Unbelievable, I know. But very true.

Years later, after Charlie no longer represented me, he put the portrait up for auction and my husband Blake Edwards found out about it and arranged for a friend to go and bid on it. So, after all that we are very happy to own it and it hangs in our home today. How prophetic that painting came to be, and to think, I wanted to chuck the whole idea.

Maya Angelou

Maya Angelou

The Heart of a Woman
By Maya Angelou
Random House, 1981

A Kept Woman I am Not!

My 1961 common-law marriage to South African political activist Vusumzi Make was for me a jarring experience. It challenged everything I had come to know about my own womanhood.

Vus was surprisingly particular about our newly apartment household in Harlem. It seemed to me that I was always thoroughly cooking, washing, scrubbing, mopping, dusting, waxing and polishing every other day. And he monitored my progress just as often. Sometimes he would pull the dresser away from the wall to see if possibly I missed a layer of dust. If he found his suspicions confirmed, his angry response would wither me. He would drop his eyes and shake his head, his eyes saddened with disappointment.

I was instructed that "a good woman" (in African accent) would create a culinary masterpiece of each meal, make-up the beds with ironed sheets and purchase toilet paper that matched the color of the bathroom tile.

I was unemployed but I had never worked so hard in all my life. Regular Monday evenings at the Harlem Writers Guild became a challenge and the best reading of the best writing could not hold my attention. When I was busted, everyone would laugh except my dearest friend Rosa Guy, who knew how hard I was trying to be a good housewife. "That African's got her jumping." Hands clapped and feet stomped at the humor of it all. But they were exposing more truth than they knew. When I wasn't home and tired, I was tights as a fist clinched in anger. My nerves were like soldiers on dress parade: sharp, erect and at attention.

We were living luxuriously but I didn't know how much cash we had, nor could I be sure that the bills were paid. He paid in cash for everything, pulling bills from a large roll of cash but the source of his money was a mystery to me. Now I was given a liberal food and house allowance and a little cash for personal expenditures. Since I had been sixteen, except for three married years between, I had earned and spent my own money. From the start, I recall how my interior decorating met with stormy disapproval. The sofa was wrong for a person of my husband's position and the second-hand store bedroom set definitely had to go.

(In African accent:) "I am an African. Even a native sleeping in the bush will lay fresh leaves on the ground. I will not sleep in a bed other man have used." I didn't ask him what he did in hotels. Certainly he didn't call the manager and say, "I want a brand new mattress. I am an African." But this novel way of life was not amusing to me and my heart was not at peace.

When Vus traveled to India for a meeting of the South African United Front, I fumbled around the house for a few days interacting with nobody by my eleven-year old son Guy. I realized I was trying my best to accommodate an uncomfortable feeling of uselessness. When every window was polished and every closet was as orderly as department store racks, I decided to go to Abbey Guy's house for a visit. The most-called upon prerequisite of a friend is an accessible ear.

"He doesn't want me to work and I don't know what's going on. It's making me feel crazy," I murmured.

Abbey brushed the nap of her couch. "You wanted a man Maya Angelou. Now you've got one." And she laughed. She didn't know how seriously troubled I was.

"But Abb, I didn't agree to give over my entire life. You know that's not right."

She locked her jaw, dropped he brow and stared at me for a long time. When she finally spoke her voice was loud and angry. "A man is supposed to be in charge, That's the order of nature, girl." She was raising an argument we had debated for years.

My position had always been that no one was responsible for my life except me. I was responsible for my son Guy only until he reached maturity, and then he had to take control over his own existence. No man had ever tried to persuade me differently by offering the security of his wealth or protection. "Well then. I must be outside of nature because I can't stand not knowing where my next air is coming from!"

Abbey made a clucking sound with her tongue and said, "The worst injury of slavery was that the white man took away the black man's right to be in charge of himself, his wife and his family. Vu is teaching you that you are not a man, no matter how strong you are or how independent you used to be. He's going to make you into an African woman. Just watch it." With that she dismissed the discussion and me. But she didn't know the African women I had met in London nor the legendary stories of African women I had heard and read. I just wanted to be a wife and create a beautiful home to make her husband happy. I was just convinced that there was more to womanhood than being a diligent maid and a permanent piece of ass.

Lauren Bacall

Lauren Bacall

Now
By Lauren Bacall
Alfred A. Knopf, 1994

Bogie's Acting Lesson

When I think about acting, I first think about my years at drama school. My first was the New York School of Theatre, which I attended on Saturdays only while I was still in high school. Then after I graduated, I was fortunate to be accepted into the "American Academy of Dramatic Arts" in its full-time program. I was taught many things but what never berates in my mind now as I reflect back almost fifty years is a single word: *technique.* I was taught to learn technique as it would become a part of me, without having to think. Then there were classes in voice (which entailed breathing, enunciation, projection and registration-meaning high-low, etc.) then body, movement, posture, timing and most importantly presence.

To me the main function of an actor is to pretend with conviction as we interpret and project the playwright's intention to the audience. I was to think that if I felt it, that would be enough, not so. It doesn't matter how much I feel it; the audience must feel it too. As I look back I can safely say I never found a formula that would enable me to get to the rest of the characters. Each one is different, each one requires an individual approach.

I am one of the few movie stars from Hollywood's middle period of filmmaking that got her start on stage and for that I am grateful. Stage work enabled me to continue working into my 60's and early 70's because movie roles are so difficult to get at that age, even if you were Lauren Bacall! And contrary to common belief, I am not rich so I need to keep working, but I believe the greatest and also the simplest acting lesson I ever learned was from Bogie himself long before we married, on the set of the Howard Hawks film of Phillip Chandler's *The Big Sleep* in 1945. One day on the set we had a scene that went like this: the doorbell rings at the stately Sternwood House, the butler goes to the door, and I (playing Vivian Sternwood) come out of my room and head for the door behind which Bogie, as Philip Marlowe is standing. On cue, I moved, could be seen emerging from the hidden room, walking toward the front door. Something went wrong, and we had to do it again. Whereupon Bogie came up to me and said, "Where are you coming from?" "My bedroom, "I said. Weren't you doing something before the doorbell rang? You don't just walk to the door because the director says "action." I have never forgotten that. Another lesson: preparation. That's what acting is, really-no breast-beating, no big motivation discussions, just thought, focus, logical thinking of where you are, where you were before, and why you are there. And listening, and truth. Most of all, acting is about telling the truth.

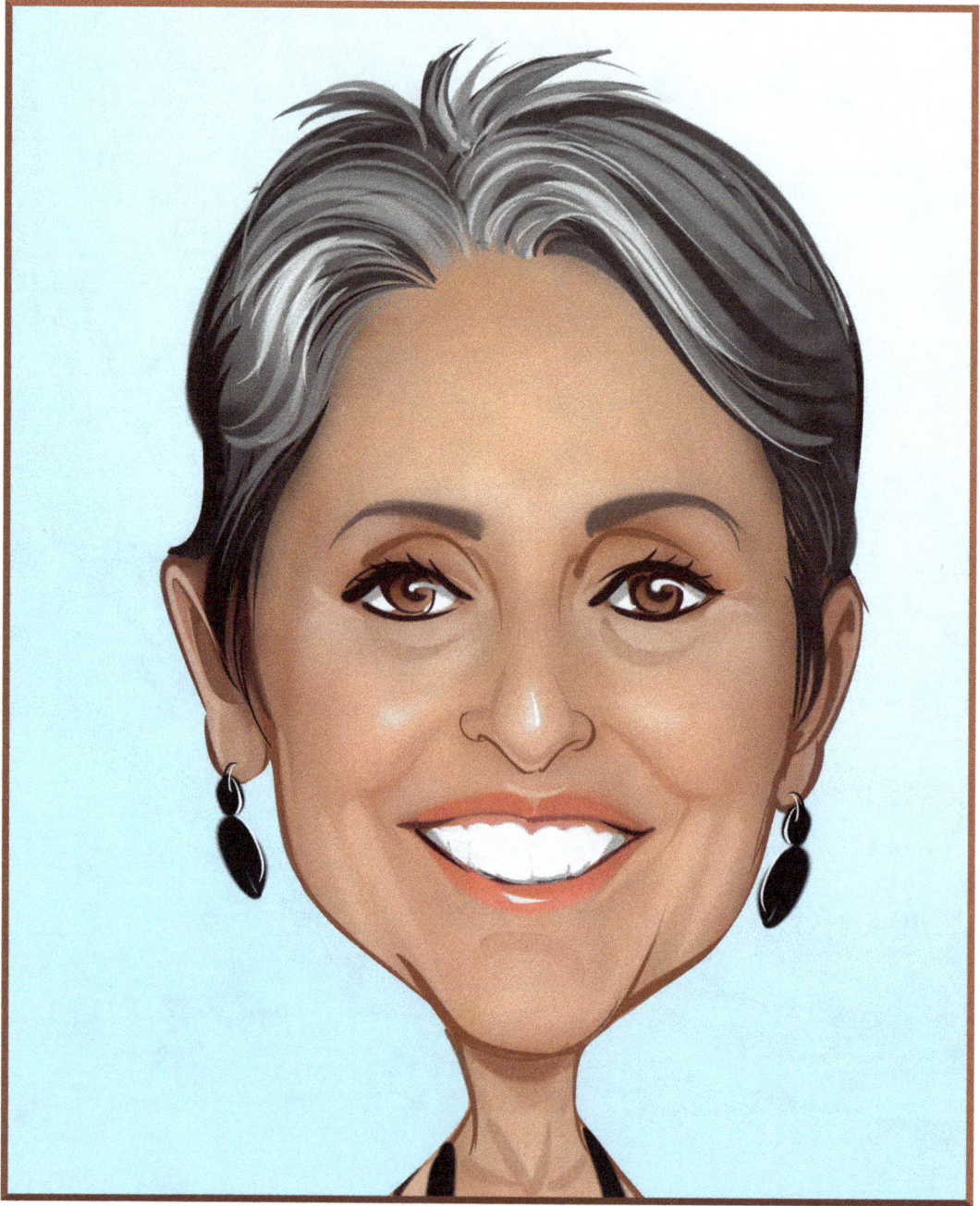

Joan Baez

Joan Baez

Daybreak
B
By Joan Baez
The Dial Press, 1968

My Baptism in Activism

I am often asked how my peace activism began. I blame it on my wonderful, thoughtful, loving and very progressive parents. They had the good sense to join a Quaker meeting house community in Oakland California where I grew up. About the only thing anybody knows about the Quakers is that they are, "we are committed" pacifists. I also blame it on the war in Vietnam, which was raging when I was in my late teens. Like with any cause in which one gets involved, there is usually one precipitating factor that more than any other reason tipped the proverbial scales in favor of my decidedly pro-peace and anti-war violence views. That would be my purely platonic relationship with the first real love of my life: a junior college instructor name Ira Sandperl. We met one boring Sunday morning in 1965 when he came to speak to our meeting house on Gandhi and non-violence.

Ira dressed in corduroys and sweatshirts and baggy duffle coat and a beat-up Alpine hat. He began to come by my house on his bicycle every morning before school. I'd skip first period and he'd be late to work and we'd walk in the morning sun and make jokes about the world, and at the same time I knew that he and I felt desperately that we must do something to try and help the world. My father asked Ira what he saw in this sixteen-year-old, to visit me every morning. Ira just told him that I was extraordinary. I began accompanying Ira to places when he spoke. I heard more things about Gandhi and love and nonviolence and a brotherhood of man, which junior high school summer camp. Ira spoke and I sang and he made some remark to the effect that we would have to travel around doing that someday and maybe we could make a change in the world.

One day I asked Ira to visit my school, Palo Alto High School. He came to an English class with me and the teacher was late, so Ira got up and began to answer questions. When the teacher arrived, we were talking about life and war and love and non-violence. The teacher had the good sense to let us continue. The administration had heard by now that English 12 had let an alligator loose in front of the kiddies and Ira and I were called to the front office at the end of the period.

The vice principal waited until the bell had rung for the next class and then he began to explain to Ira how it was illegal for him to be on the campus without a certain pink pass signed by the principal. I asked him if he could please give us one and he said no he could not, that it had to be applied for by one of the students and then decided upon by the administration and would I please go to my class now. I asked him why I should go to my class, and he said because the bell had rung. I said I was staying until my guest left and the vice-principal said no, no, go back to class; how could I learn anything if I didn't go to class. I told him I was learning something right that minute. I was learning how he and Ira acted with each other.

He gave up and just tried to hurry Ira out the door. I took Ira's arm and walked him out of the office and down the hall to the front entrance. I knew the vice-principal was peeking from somewhere, so I walked out of the building onto the porch just to give him a scare and I shook Ira's hand good-bye. I don't know why I didn't keep walking, I would have been right. The only real teacher at school that day was being kicked off the campus.

Roseanne Barr

Roseanne Barr

My Life as a Woman
By Rosanne Barr
Harper & Row, 1989

A Lesson in Honesty

When I was five years old and we lived across the street from a little grocery store, and mother allowed me to go over there all by myself, which meant, of course that she would stand there and make sure all the traffic had subsided and then, like a track coach, scream, "alright, go"! While I was going, she would scream, "Run! Run!" like it was the end of the world. I did not cross a street without her until I was nine years old. When I came back and handed mother her purchase, she noticed I'd been given $1.00 too much in change and decided to educate me as to the wise and crucial ways of being honest and god-fearing and right thinking and all, but because it was very cold outside, I refused to go back, mother then drilled into me that our heavenly father was watching and would like it if I took back the dollar. Thus, properly induced into religious ecstasy, turning to returning the excess loot, I slipped on the ice and all of my upper teeth went cleanly and fully through my lips; I was rushed to the hospital, laid on a table, covered with a sheet from head to toe and underwent ninety minutes of surgery.

The wonderful lesson about honesty and doing the right thing was planted into my consciousness. I learned that not even God himself likes "ass kissers".

Candice Bergen

Candice Bergen

A Fine Romance
By Candice Bergen
Simon & Schuster, 2015

The Red Carpet Game

*I*n Los Angeles from the month of September on, it's one infernal awards show after another. Emmys, Golden Globes, SAG Awards, Independent Spirit, Oscars and others. You start getting ready at 11:00 a.m., leave home by 2:00 p.m. in full makeup, borrowed jewels, and a gown. You're finished in time for dinner. It takes a village: hair and tanning people, manicurists, makeup, and personal stylists, obviously. They are called your team. The studio pays for it. Thank God!

The Red Carpet is a grotesque marketplace. A celebrity souk filled with publicists, press, police, and fans. Most people of a certain age try to do it with as much grace as possible, to be as genuine as possible under the most artificial construct. Most fail.

The press line over time has grown longer and deeper, stretching for blocks. During my *Murphy Brown* years, I was always ushered through the scrum by two studio publicists, each of whom would take turns playing good cop-bad cop as they kept me moving through the line. They knew who was important, who wasn't; for whom and for how long I should stop and how I should pose. They understood it was an ordeal but that it was a necessary part of the game. I'd go from one lame-brained interview to the next.

"What's the difference between you and your character?"

"How much does it mean to you?"

"Who did your hair?" "Whose gown are you wearing?"

And the importance of displaying my "gifts" such as my handbag, my gown, my jewelry, gracefully. Today, everything is a gift from the designers. If you're smart, you don't need to spend a shekel, as long as you are photographed in it, on it or with it.

When I started *Murphy Brown*, stylists didn't really exist. In those days, I knew many designers and I would call their PR people and they were always lovely. They would let me keep the gowns I wore, and I would be thrilled and send them a thank you note, flowers or an engraved gift of something nice. But when professional stylists emerged on the scene, I started working with one named Jane Ross. Once she found me a Bill Blass to wear to the Emmys. It was a dark gold strapless gown with russet cut-velvet jacquard. With it she matched canary diamond earrings, emerald cut and chic as hell. Sometimes Jane would pull pieces worth hundreds of thousands of dollars out of her pockets. If it was worth even more, the jewelry was delivered by security guards to my door with a form to be signed.

These days you find a lot of women who really know how to work the Red Carpet. They are pros, nonchalantly giving photographers twelve positions: the coy over-the-shoulder-with-the-backless shot; the hip-forward-cocked-thigh-in-the-slinky-slit dress shot; the shoulders-back-so-you-don't-see-her-nipples shot; and other such looks which are so routine today. My favorites are the look that says you can't believe they let you into the game, and the look that says you can't wait to get out.

Benazir Bhutto

Benazir Bhutto

Daughter of Destiny
By Benazir Bhutto
HarperCollins, 2007

Prime Minister and Pregnant

Shortly after I was elected Prime Minster of Pakistan in 1989, my mother told me to hurry up and have a second child. She believed that a woman should quickly have children before she realized the challenges of raising a family and fulfilling life's other responsibilities. I took her advice.

When I was expecting my first child two years before, the then military dictator dismissed the Parliament and called for general elections. He and his top army lieutenants believed a pregnant woman could not possibly campaign. They were wrong. I could and I did. I went on to win the elections and took office while I was still breast-feeding my son.

While my second pregnancy was still a secret, my generals decided to take me to the Siachen Glaciers, the highest point in Pakistan, for a military briefing. Pakistan and India had nearly gone to war over Siachen only a year before (and then again ten years later). I was worried that the thin air on those mountain peaks could adversely affect my unborn baby. My doctor assured me I could go but advised me to take an oxygen mask in case I felt dizzy or nauseous. So, with much trepidation despite his assurance that it was not unsafe, I went on the mission.

It was a splendid site and my visit was a great morale-booster for our troops. All around us and as far as one could see, was the frigid whiteness of the icy glaciers, which melted seamlessly into the blueness of the sky. The absence of earthy noise on those snowy peaks gave new meaning to heavenly silence. Across the divide I could see the Indian military posts in the distance. They proved to me that the appearance of peace and quiet could be deceptive.

After my secret was revealed, the political opposition went all out to unseat me. They called upon the president and the military to overthrow me. They argued that during delivery I would be incapacitated and that the government would be at a standstill while I was on maternity leave. In an effort to defeat common stereotypes, I worked extra hard to convince those around me that I was perfectly capable of being with child and remain competent. Thankfully, the members of my cabinet and party stood by me, replying that when a male leader was indisposed, it did not translate into a political crisis. Hardly mollified, the opposition drew up a plan for countrywide labor strikes to cripple the economy and pressure the president to sack my government. Remembering my father's advice about timing in politics, I consulted my doctor again and, being that I was near full term, decided to have a Caesarian delivery on the eve the strike action was scheduled to begin.

As soon as I began to wake from the mists of the anesthesia as I was being wheeled to my room, I heard my husband say, "It's a girl." I remember seeing my mother with him, her face beaming with pleasure. I decided to call my daughter Bahktwar, which means one who brings good fortune. And she did. The strike plan fizzled out and the opposition's movement quickly collapsed. The next day I was back on the job, taking meetings, reading reports and signing off on state matters. Only later did I learn that I was the only head of government in recorded history to give birth while in office. That's one less glass ceiling for female leaders of the future to have to shatter. As a woman I was proud; as a Muslim I was even prouder.

Mika Brzezinski

Mika Brzezinski

All Things at Once
By Mika Brezezinski
Weinstein Books, 2009

Makeover and Over

Television is obviously a visual medium – much more so for women than for men. This in itself is hardly breaking news, but it is worth emphasizing here. In the broadcast news business there is constant pressure for on-air talent to "look good." It takes up an awful lot of our time – far too much, if you ask me. And yet, whether or not we choose to buy into it, our "look" is an important part of our package. It's just as important as our knowledge, our insights, our experience and our ability to tell a story.

I found it exhausting trying to keep up with the latest fashions, hairdos and makeup – not to mention paying attention to my figure. I didn't do a very good job of managing my image, especially early in my career. A part of me didn't know enough to understand it was so vital to success. During most of my run at the CBS News overnight broadcast, I looked haggard and worn and probably overweight. I found it impossible not to look bone-tired. Plus, I overate to stay awake – an occupational hazard – and the fact for most of my time there I was either pregnant or nursing didn't exactly inspire an enticing look. Add to that the rinky-dink lighting in our fifth-floor studio, which was more like the lighting in a fifth-grade classroom and my worst features were highlighted for all America to witness. I was forced to perform a makeover and frankly, I resented it but knew it was mandatory.

Looks matter. They just do. They go into the toolbox every on-air journalist must carry about with them. It's often how we market and position ourselves on the air, and at the same time it's also how we sell ourselves to news managers and network executives, who use their own subjective "tastes" coupled with perceived demographics to make hiring decisions. I learned this firsthand, a few times too many. Sometimes managers are quite blunt about this; sometimes they are vague and evasive; but always they are inclined to make a safe decision and go with talent who is easy on the eyes.

My big break at MSNBC came with another complete makeover. A female vice president called in a team of stylists and they took me on a whirlwind shopping spree. We went up and down Fifth Avenue, buying up the town – to the tune of $25,000 I was told. Then they took me to a high-end salon. It was nuts, almost like a bride getting ready for her wedding. I didn't mind all the fuss, but I felt a little uneasy with the look they had envisioned. It was not a look I would have chosen for myself. I suppose that was exactly their purpose. I figured they knew what they were doing. They proceeded to outfit me in short skirts, high boots, and tight-fitting sleeveless tops. They transformed me into a blonde. I have to admit, compared with my "before" my "after" looked great. That's what a makeover intervention can do for you when it is coupled with some much-needed rest and pampering. But if didn't "look" like me and for a time afterward I had to wrestle with the feeling I was a phony.

Carol Burnett

Carol Burnett

One More Time
By Carol Burnett
Random House, 1986

My Imaginary Twin Sister

My school friend Asher used to sit on the couch in the lobby of the motel where we lived and read comic books. He wore thick eyeglasses and his face was always hidden by the cover of those books, he was younger than I and a cinch to fool. I had him thinking I was twins for two whole days. One day I walked right past him and into our room #102 which faced the lobby. Nobody was home and I was bored. I changed my clothes, grabbed an old suitcase we had, climbed out the window, ran around the back of the building to the front, and walked into the lobby again.

You see, I had thought up a way to entertain myself, it was inspired. I approached him and asked in a crude English accent, where Carol lived. He looked up from a Batman comic and did a double take. He then pointed to our door and I opened it and walked right in before he could say another word. I then held a loud conversation with myself behind the door, making sure he could hear every word. "Oh my God!" You're here. You look wonderful!" I followed these enthusiastic exclamations with shrieks and screams of delight, "How long can you stay? Oh, how I've missed you." Back and forth it went, and all this time I was frantically changing my clothes and getting back into "Carol," all while trying to sound like two separate girls. After I finished changing, I jumped out into the lobby and told Asher that my twin sister Karen has just this minute arrived from …. Canada.

By now he had put down his comic book and found his voice. "Gosh, I never knew you had a twin sister!" "O yes, we were separated at birth. But don't tell anybody, it's a secret and I will get in big trouble if my mom finds out I told you," I looked down at the floor as if it hurt too much to talk, "Asher," I said, "please don't ask me any questions, I, I've said too much as it is."

There was a silent moment, and I seized it to run dramatically out the front door of the building, leaving him to think I might be heading straight into traffic or something. But I ran around the back of the building again, and this time I climbed back into the window of the room #102. I changed my clothes and became once again Karen. I waited a couple of minutes and then opened the door and looked around the lobby. Asher's mouth was still wide open.

"Excuse me but have you seen Carol?" He said sheepishly. He stood there and stared at me. I was beginning to wonder if he'd ever blinked again. Finally he said, "I didn't know Carol had a twin." I stared back at him with my most pained expression I could summon, made my chin quiver, ran back into my room and slammed the door. I sobbed just loud enough to trouble him.

Back into Carol, out the window, around the building and into the lobby. I was beginning to feel a little tired. I spent the rest of the afternoon changing my clothes, my voice and running around the building. He bought the whole thing and I dad a swell time. I let my girlfriend Amy in on my scheme the next day and she played right along. She helped out by telling Asher she had known about Karen for a long time, but it was a deep dark family secret and he'd better keep it to himself or else.

He even crossed his heart and hoped to die. That afternoon was pretty much a repeat of the day before. I had both him and I going around in circles. But after a couple of hours of climbing out and in the window, running around the building and all the while holding mock conversations with myself while frantically changing clothes, I got a little careless. After a while, instead of changing clothes, I put on an old chenille robe over what I was wearing as "Karen." Asher spotted what I had on underneath it. I had forgotten there was a big hole in the sleeve of the robe. I tried to bluff my way out but it was all over. I was exhausted . . . but I was an actress.

Barbara Bush

Barbara Bush

A Memoir
By Barbara Bush
Scribners/Simon & Schuster, 1994

The Symbolic Antique Door

As footnote to our victory against Iraqi forces in Desert Storm: George and I went to Kuwait in March 1993, a little more than a month after we left the White House. We were invited as guests of the Kuwait government. It was an extraordinary trip, and I wish all the families who lost loved ones could have been with us to experience the depth of gratitude the Kuwait's expressed. It was actually overwhelming. People waived American and Kuwaiti flags for mile after mile everywhere we went, and the Arab women always made that wonderful and distinct guttural shrill to celebrate our presence. People stood for hours just to catch a glimpse of George whose face was everywhere on posters, flags and billboards.

We saw such devastation and heard tales of horror and cruelty, we met with families whose sons and husbands were missing in action or still held as hostages in Iraq. We saw museums and government buildings that were torched the last two days of the war, so senselessly. We heard of ropes, beatings and torture and visited a hospital where the handicapped were thrown out on the streets to make way for wounded Iraqi soldiers and whose maternity ward equipment was looted and taken back to Iraq, including incubators and entire operating rooms. Everyone we met had a death of a family member to lament.

We also visited the blackened and stench-filled oil fields where eventually over seven hundred wells had been set on fire as the vanquished and retreating Iraq Army spitefully fled the country. However, all the suffering and destruction reminded me that nature and the human spirit are amazing. We saw rebuilding everywhere. We experienced genuine optimism and faith in the future by a cross-section of the Kuwaite people. There were even patches of plant life shooting through the thin layer of oil that covered the ground. I even saw some resilient yellow wildflowers and I was told the oil actually aided their growth by preserving what little moisture was still in the soil.

We went one morning to visit with families of POW'S and MIA'S and they presented George with a beautifully carved antique door, as we approached it, we were moved to see that they had inscribed on the door in gold the names of all the American men and women killed freeing their country. Above the names was inscribed the following: "When a man gives you the key to his home, it means you are the best and most valuable friend to him; but when he gives you the door to his house it means that you are one of his family."

This beautiful old door symbolized to us more than anything their gratitude and it will forever be on display at the George Bush Presidential Library Center in College Station, Texas for all to see and to always honor those courageous Americans who gave their lives in that valiant effort.

Laura Bush

Laura Bush

Spoken from the Heart
By Laura Bush
Scribner, 2010

Our first state dinner was held to honor the visit of Tony and Cherie Blair of the United Kingdom. Earlier that day, I enjoyed a visit with Oprah Winfrey and her friend and business partner, Gayle King. There was tremendous curiosity about me in those first few weeks and I had received countless requests for interviews. I was pleased to grant Oprah the first one.

I was upstairs I our White House living quarters, still getting things organized while I waited for Oprah and Gayle to arrive. Unbeknownst to me, George passed by with Condoleezza Rice, his national security advisor, and Colin Powell, his secretary of state. My staff later told me that Oprah was speechless at meeting them. For the first time, the two individuals tasked with overseeing U.S. foreign policy were African-Americans. Gayle had to give Oprah a little poke to remind her to begin the interview.

And I thought later, what a wonderful moment to have this crossroads of success in the people's house that was, at the founding the nation, built by the hard labor of so many unknown and unrecognized slaves. I felt proud and hoped this pride would remain with me for the coming years. I'm happy to report that it mostly did.

Julia Child

Julia Childs

My Life in France
By Julia Childs
Alfred A. Knopf, 2006

My Husband Paul

As a girl I had zero interest in cooking. I've always had a healthy appetite, especially for the wonderful beauty of Pasadena. Our family had a succession of hired cooks so I just didn't see the point of it and I was never encouraged to give cooking a try. Our meals were ordinary American face – hearty, delicious but not refined dishes.

I met my late husband Paul Childs while we both worked for the OSS – now the CIA – in Ceylon – now Sri Lanka – during the last year of World War II. We were married in September 1946 and in preparation for living together on a limited government salary, I decided that I better learn my way around the kitchen. Before our wedding, I enrolled in a ten-week cooking course offered by two British women living in Los Angeles. But all I learned were the basics, like how to make pancakes, bake bread and jar preserves for the winter. The first meal I ever cooked for Paul was more ambitious: cow brains simmered in red wine. I'm not quite sure why I picked that particular dish, other than that it sounded exotic and could be a fun way to impress him.

I skimmed over the recipe and concluded that it would be easy and cheap to prepare. But the results, alas, were messy to look at and even worse to eat. In fact, the whole dinner was a disaster. Paul laughed it off and we scrounged up something else to eat. But deep down I was annoyed with myself, and it was that evening that I grew more determined than ever to learn how to cook well.

I was lucky to marry Paul. He was always a great inspiration and his enthusiasm about wine and foods helped me change my tastes, and his encouragement saw me through discouraging moments. I would never had my career without Paul Childs.

Hillary Clinton

Hillary Clinton

Living History
by Hillary Rodham Clinton
Simon & Schuster, 2003

Boris Yelstin and Moose Lip Soup

Whenever we traveled abroad, the State Department always gave us fact sheets about the countries we visited, along with helpful protocol hints. Sometimes I was warned about unusual foods I might be served and how I could avoid eating them without insulting my host. One veteran foreign service officer suggested I should "push the food around" on the plate to simulate consumption, a trick well-known to every five-year old. But no diplomatic manual could possibly have prepared me for my dining experiences with Boris Yeltsin and I considered him a true hero who saved democracy twice in Russia: first when he climbed onto a tank in Red Square in 1991 and spoke out in defiance of the military coup attempt and again in 1993, when a military cabal tried to take over the Russian White House and Yeltsin stood firmly for democracy, aided by strong support from Bill and other world leaders. He is also, in his own way delightful company. He has a great heart and can always make me laugh. Of course, he has a reputation for being unpredictable, and as often apparent, he enjoys his vodka, whiskey and wine.

I was usually seated next to Yeltsin at official dinners, and his wife Naina was seated next to Bill. He did not speak English, but a simultaneous translator sitting behind us conveyed his words to Bill and me in the same deep, raspy voice and with all of Boris's inflections. Boris rarely touched his food as each course was set before us, he'd push it away or ignore it while continuing to tell us stories. Sometimes the food itself became a story.

When the Yeltsin's hosted us at the brand-new Russian embassy in Washington in September 1994, Bill and I were seated with them on a dais before dozens of tables filled with luminaries from Washington society as well a Russian and U.S. officials. Suddenly Yeltsin motioned Bill and me to lean toward him. *"Heel-larg!"*, he said. Bill! Look at those people out there. You know what they are thinking? They all are thinking, "how could Boris and Bill be up there and not us?" This was a telling comment. Yeltsin was smarter than some of his adversaries understood, and he was well-aware of the whispering campaign from the Kremlin to the State Department that he was not acceptable or polished enough. He also knew that some of the same people disapproved of Bill's exuberance and looked down upon his Arkansas roots. We smiled and picked up our forks, but Yeltsin kept going. "Hahhh!" He laughed and turned to the president. "I have a treat for you Bill!"

A whole stuffed piglet was laid out on the table in front of us. With one swipe of his knife, Yeltsin sliced off an ear and handed it to my husband. He cut the other ear for himself, raised it to his mouth and bit off a piece, gesturing for Bill to do the same.

"To us," he said, holding up the remainder of the ear as though it were a glass of fine champagne. It's a good thing Bill Clinton has an iron stomach. His ability to eat anything put in front of him is one of his many political talents. I do not share his intestinal fortitude and Yeltsin knew it. He loved to tease me, and this was one moment when I was glad that a sow has only two ears.

Years later, toward the end of Yeltsin's and Bill's terms in office, we had one final dinner together in the Kremlin. It was held in the domed St. Catherine Hall, one of the loveliest of the ornate dining halls in the old palace. Toward the middle of the meal, Yeltsin said to me in his rumbling, conspiratorial voice, *"Heel-larg!* I will miss seeing you. I have a picture of you in my office, I look at it every day". There was a mischievous gleam in his eye. Well, "thank you Boris" I said. "I hope we will still see each other from time to time." "Good", he said.

"Now Hillary, I have a very special treat for you tonight. What is it? I'm not going to tell you! You must wait until it comes"! We sat through course after course and toast after toast and finally, just before dessert, a waiter set bowls of hot soup in front of us. "This is it Hillary your special treat," said Boris, grinning as he sniffed the pungent steam. "Mmm! Delicious!"

"What is it"? I asked as I picked up my spoon. He paused dramatically. "Moose lips"! Sure enough, floating in the murky broth was my own set of moose lips. The gelatinous shapes looked like rubber bands that had lost their stretch, and I pushed them around the bowl until the waiter took them away. I've tasted a lot of unusual food for my country, but I draw the line at moose lips.

Joan Collins

Joan Collins

Second Act
By Joan Collins
St. Martin's Press, 1996

Glimpses of Elizabeth Taylor

I'd known and liked Elizabeth Taylor for years. We'd often run into each other at Hollywood events and private parties. And yes, she was notoriously late every time. Shortly after I'd arrived in Los Angeles we'd double-dated at the very trendy La Rue restaurant, and had chattered away girlishly. She is, like Natalie Wood and Marilyn Monroe had been, a girl's girl. Many people would disagree and believe she is more a man's woman. But there is no bitchiness, envy or venom in Elizabeth as there is in so many other, lesser Hollywood women. If she likes you, she genuinely likes you and lets you know you have a fiend for life. Throughout the years our paths had continued to cross. For example, I'd dated her first ex-husband, the dissolute Nicky Hilton and she had dated my former boyfriend Arthur Loew Jr. I was chosen to be her understudy during the filming of *Cleopatra* and was asked to be ready to take over for her when she came down with a nasty case of pneumonia in Italy where it was made. I'd also attended a dreadful dinner party at the opulent Roman villa she and her husband Eddie Fisher held, and watched with a group of horrified acquaintances as she berated him for being drunk. But by that time she was already in love with Richard Burton and probably looking for a respectable way out since that marriage was such a major scandal because of the way she jilted the lovely Debbie Reynolds, then a young mother and the darling of wholesome society. Everyone knew about Liz and Dick then, except Eddie.

Once when she was late in arriving at my home for a viewing party of the first episode of my TV series *Monte Carlo*, she was impeccably dressed and coiffed. She was watching her weight and wouldn't eat so she smoked cigarettes instead. When she struck a match awkwardly, her acrylic fingernail caught on fire and George Hamilton, my co-star, dosed her had with a martini. She went upstairs to my room to fix it and rejoined us without a hint of distress and everybody was relieved.

We also had several friends in common and before her fiftieth birthday party (which she threw for herself in her Bel Air estate), I'd asked them, "What do you buy for a woman who has everything?" It was no secret she adored receiving gifts and I decided to give he a Victorian silver picture frame. But she also loves giving gifts too and is extremely generous to her friends. When I was getting married, a large box beautifully wrapped in lilac-scented paper arrived from the most exclusive linen shop in Beverly Hills. Inside was a gorgeous peach cashmere blanket embroidered with our initials. Unbelievably luxurious, it was one of the most expensive wedding gifts we received. Written on a card in violet ink was a message of love and congratulations. It's obvious Elizabeth likes seeing her friends get married almost as much as she likes doing it herself.

Ellen DeGeneres

Ellen DeGeneres

Seriously...I'm Kidding
By Ellen DeGeneres
Grand Central Publishing, 2011

That's How Prejudice Begins

Unfortunately, I get labeled a lot, I'm often labeled as a "gay talk show host" or a "vegan animal lover" or "a dancing superstar the likes of which this world has never seen before." I remember after I became a "Cover Girl," people started labeling me as just another "gorgeous blonde model with a pretty face" and they stopped taking me seriously. That was really hard. The problem with labels is that leads to stereotypes and stereotype lead back to stereotypes. That's how prejudice begins. It's a vicious cycle, and after you go around and around a bunch times, you end up believing that all vegans only eat greens and all gay people love musicals.

Stereotypes obviously come from somewhere. There are similarities among certain groups of people, but it would be dangerous to assume all stereotypes are accurate. You can't say all blondes are dumb or all white men can't jump. Nor can you say all rich people are snobs or all celebrities have inflated egos. But going back to me for a moment, I accept that there are a lot of stereotypes associated with being gay. However, I didn't realize just how many there are until recently when a woman asked me how many cats I have. When I told her I have three, the first thing she said was, "Oh, you really are a lesbian!" And at first I thought, "Well yes I really am; that secret's been out for many years." But then I thought, "What, what? When did the number of cats one has become a stereotype?" I always thought that people who have a lot of cats are simply single and lonely. Oops, that's another stereotype.

I was so taken back by her comment. How does the number of cats you have make one a lesbian? And why is three the lesbian number? Would having just two cats mean I'm straight? Would having four make me a bisexual? When she said that, it reminded me of when I came out. At that time there were extremist groups that didn't think I was gay enough. And there were other groups of people that thought I was too gay. It had never occurred to me that when I announced I was gay, I would have to clarify just how gay I am. What does it mean? What does it matter? All I can say is I am gay enough for me.

To me, that's why stereotypes and labels can be so damaging. People make these sweeping generalizations and have preconceived notions of what you're supposed to be and of who you are based upon a few tiny words. I believe it's important to actually get to know someone before you make such generalizations. And you can do that pretty easily just by talking to them, asking them questions or secretly reading their diary. Despite all the labels, in most ways I'm not really that different from anyone else. I guess if you had to label me, you could say I'm like the girl next door. Well, maybe not next door. I'm more like the girl at the end of the block.

Fran Drescher

Fran Drescher

Enter Whining
By Fran Drescher
Regan Books, 1996

My Queer Fans

Once, on a trip to New York, my husband and I decided we would try to get tickets for Barbara Streisand's show at Madison Square Garden, tickets that were extremely difficult to get. We were told by a Sony executive that she records under the Sony label and that Sony signatures was handling all the merchandising as well. Before we could say "evergreen," two ground floor-level complimentary tickets were messengered to our hotel. This really takes the cake. We're going to hear Streisand sing live, "Somebody pinch me, we're not worthy, were not worthy," we thought as we melted into the thousands of paying customers at the Garden's entrance.

What an exciting night: the thrill, the rush, the fans are beginning to notice me. Soon, everywhere we turned, large groups were looking, pointing, and moving toward me. It never occurred to me but my husband Peter said, "We're in New York at a Streisand concert." I guess a lot of her fans are your fans too! Who knew? Then we learned it was Gay Pride Week and that explained everything, including running into Bette Midler at a party afterwards.

Lena Dunham

Lena Dunham

Not that Kind of Girl:
A Young Woman Tells What She's "Learned"
By Lena Dunham
Random House, 2014

I've Been Obsessed with Death Since I was Born

I think a fair amount about the fact that we're all going to die. It occurs to me at incredibly inopportune moments. I'll be standing in a bar, having managed to get an attractive guy to laugh, and I'll be laughing too and maybe dancing a little bit, and then everything goes slo-mo for a second and I'll think: Are these people aware that we are all going to the same place in the end?

I can slip back into conversation and tell myself that the flash of mortality aware-ness has enriched my life experience, reminded to just go for it in the giggling and hair-flipping and speaking-my-mind departments because …well why the hell not? But occasionally the feeling stays with me, and it reminds me of being a child, feeling full of fear but lacking the language to calm myself down. I guess, when it comes to death none of us really has the words to do it.

The hypochondria. The Intensity of my reactions to death, and my inability to disengage from the topic once it is raised. My need to make it clear to everyone that it is coming for them, too. My need to meditate on it. Is what's manifesting as a fear actually some instinct to resist being young? Youth, with all its risks, humiliations and uncertainties, the pressure to do it all before it's too late. Is the preoccupation of imminent death bound up in some need to leave a legacy?

I am still in my twenties, so a fear of death is, while reasonable in a macro way, also irrational. Most people live through their twenties. And their thirties. And their forties. Many people even live longer than is amusing, even to them. So, every time I think about being dead, like when I am lying in bed and imagine disintegrating, my skin going leathery and my hair petrifying and a tree growing out of my stomach, it's a way to avoid what's right in front of me. It's a way not to be here, in the uncertainty of the right now.

Sarah Ferguson

Sarah Ferguson

Sarah, The Duchess of York: My Story
By Sarah Ferguson with Jeff Coplon
Simon and Schuster, 1996

On Being a Royal

To be a proper royal duchess is more than a fulltime job. Modern royalty is expected to sing for its supper, to earn its keep. Each day, at the back of *The Times* and the *Daily Telegraph*, the post a feature called "Court Circular," which is a listing of the prior day's engagements for each member of the royal family. Sadly, in practice it turns into a competition, a kind of numbers game. The press keeps a running tabulation and is all too gleeful to point out when someone lags in the standings. Royal, work has three components: official engagements, charity engagements, and high ceremonies like Remembrance Day or Trooping the Colours.

Andrew and I were scheduled six months in advance, based on joint household meetings in December and June, when our top staff people would excavate through mounds of invitations and recommend the ones they thought best. There was no set pecking order with in the Royal Family as to what you could do, but it was understood that one didn't raid existing franchises. Princess Anne, for example, had cornered the market on "Save the Children," Princess Margaret had tied up the National Society for Prevention of Cruelty to Children; Prince Charles had an exclusive on Architecture, Environment and Urban Affairs. In the main you could follow your preferences – if you met the unwritten quota. Accordingly, I decided to focus my efforts on Animal Cruelty and Childhood Obesity. Working against them that is.

Tina Fey

Tina Fey

Bossypants
By Tina Fey
Little Brown & Co., 2011

I Am a Working Mom

My daughter recently checked out a book from the pre-school library titled, "My working mom". It had a cartoon witch on the cover. "Did you pick this book out all by yourself?" I asked her, trying to be nonchalant. "Yes". We read the story and the witch mother was very busy and sometimes reprimanded her little witch daughter from paying too close to their cauldron. She had to use her broomstick to fly to a lot of meetings and the little witch said something like, "It's hard to have a working mom, especially when she enjoys her job." In the heartwarming conclusion, the busy witch mother just makes it to her daughter's school day. It's a happy ending because while the little witch says she doesn't like having a working mom she can't picture her mom any other way. I'm sure the two men who wrote and illustrated this story had the absolute best intentions, but this leads me to my point. The topic of working moms is a top-dance recital in a minefield.

It is less dangerous to draw a cartoon of Mohammed kissing Uncle Sam which let me make very clear I have never done-than it is to speak honestly about this topic. I will start by saying that I have more than once been offered a "mother of the year" award by working mom groups or woman's magazines and I always decline. How could they possibly know what kind of mother I am? How can any of us know until the kid (or kids) are in their mid-thirties and all their personality dust has settled?But working moms need to validate that it's okay to work, especially if they work at trendy magazines where they can package that validation and sell it to stay-at-home moms who are craving for stories from the other side. "How do you juggle it all?" People constantly ask me, often with a suspicious look in their eyes. "You're fucking it all up, aren't you?" they are really asking. My standard reply is that I face the same struggles as any other working parent but I have the good fortune to earn a lot of money at a dream job, and that makes all the difference. But of course the long version of the answer is more complicated.

When my daughter was about two, I was convinced – no – obsessed that our babysitter Jessie (Note: I refuse to call her a "nanny") was clipping her fingernails too short. Now I can tell twenty cynical comedy writers what to do. I can argue with the most hardened New York City cabbie; I will happily tell a joke about al-Qaeda on national TV but for some bizarre reason, I could not bring myself to speak to Jessie about her fingernail clipping practices. But here's the truth: I couldn't bring myself to tell the woman who so lovingly and devotedly cares for my kid every day that I didn't like the way she did this one thing, I just didn't want to hurt her feelings.

Now here's the deeper truth: I didn't want to spend my precious at home time having an awkward discussion with my babysitter about what I feared she would regard as a petty thing. So what did I do about my daughter's finger nails? I did the logical thing of course – I made a game out of it. First thing in the morning while she was on the potty, I would clip her nails before I left for work. The process was preposterously slow but we huddled together and exchanged laughs as we went along. This is one of the weird things about motherhood. You can't predict that some of your best moments will occur at the toilet before six a.m. while you're holding a pile of fingernail (and toenail) clippings like a Santeria priestess.

It's three years later now, I'd like to believe my household communication skills have improved. For example, I can now whisper to my five-year old daughter, "Tell Jessie not to trim your nails too short. Bye!" and run away. My daughter and I can have real communications now. I told her I didn't like it when she selected a story book in which the mommy was a witch, that it hurt my feelings. She looked at me matter-of-factly and said, "Mommy, I thought it was a Halloween book."

Carrie Fisher

Carrie Fisher

Shockaholic
By Carrie Fisher
Simon & Schuster, 2011

My Impression of Michael Jackson

I did not know Michael Jackson that well but in the climate that developed in the wake of his death, to not have known him well was, for some, enough to be seen as having known him intimately. And from this certain skewed slant, I could even be perceived as one of Michael's closest friends. He and I had just two people in common: Elizabeth Taylor, who we all know, and Arnold Klein, our dermatologist. He was known as the Dermatologist to the Stars and is singularly responsible for the popularity of Botox injections. And as we all know, Michael had a thing about his skin. He and Liz were close but he and Michael were even closer, so close that Michael chose one of Dr. Klein's nurses to be the mother of his first two children. Yes, I know, a very strange way to demonstrate trust, but there you have it. And Michael wanted access to the farthest reaches of medical care 24-7, at a speed and ease that eventually lead to his tragic and untimely death.

To be sure, Michael was very unusual. For one thing, his relationship to his appearance was … let's be kind and call it atypical. That he could have consistently hammered away at his perfectly nice original face until he arrived at that strange place he paused at – that place where he was able to look in the mirror and essentially say to himself, "Yes, this is the face I'm more comfortable with." The word "dysmorphic" doesn't even begin to cover it. He was, to say the least, out of the ordinary – miles out there. Somewhere that leaves ordinary far behind. But to be such a distance from ordinary makes you a singular sort of person. And Michael certainly was that. Peerless, unlike any other.

He was so distinctively "other." He possessed qualities that very few others could lay claim to Some qualities that few would wish for, but others that to some would seem blessed. He could move – and move others – like no other. He altered any room he was in. Which could not only make one want to be in his room but perhaps also want to make one stay out.

My six-year old daughter Billie and I had the good fortune of spending the weekend at Neverland, not at Michael's invitation, but at Dr. Klein's. Michael trusted him enough to let him have full charge there and let him invite as many guests as he wanted. So, we gathered in Michael's vast manicured acreage, on which was ensconced a neat cluster of guest houses complete with their own gift bars of Neverland soap. I coveted that soap; I stole that soap; I lost that soap.

When Billie was about six months old, Michael saw some of her pictures on the wall of Dr. Klein's office. He called me and left a message, asking for a photo of Billie. Now, that was odd. But you know, considering that this was years before all the allegations against him, I thought is was kind of sweet. It was like he identified with or was drawn to innocent things. And yet everyone turned that into something perverse. No one could believe he was *that* innocent but I actually did.

Michael's celebrity turned many people into eager, greedy stargazers who only wanted something from him above and beyond what a normal person is willing or expected to give. They were there for the anecdote. It's what I call the "shine."

People want to rub up against it, and in so doing, their own self-worth is increased. I'd like to propose my own theory why I believe Michael preferred the company of children to what I have referred to as adults.

Kids of a certain age don't understand fame. They just weren't that impressed by him for who he is supposed to be and accepted him for exactly who he was, a little kid himself. Alternately, the only others who were not beguiled by fame are those who are just as famous, which I believe was essentially the recipe that kept him glued to Liz Taylor. When they were together it was shine -squared. I believe he was no more sexual with those kids, inappropriate as his conduct was, than he was with Liz. Odd as it sounds, I actually don't think Michael was sexual at all. Sexy yes, sexual no. There is a big difference and we too often confuse the two, much to our detriment. And in Michael's case, to his inconsolable shame.

Connie Francis

Connie Francis

Who's Sorry Now?
By Connie Francis
St. Martin's Press, 1984

Dick Clark's Magic Touch

One day, with the flick of a switch, I became a star. The day started off like every other New Year's Day I could remember, with festivity in the air, a ton of relatives, and enough of aunt Ida's food to feed Ecuador. But, it would prove to be unlike all the rest. This January first marked the beginning of a totally new life for me-one that would never be the same. Precisely at 4:00 pm, I excused myself from the dinner table, like 8.5 million other loyal teenagers, I turned on our black and white 16 inch Motorola to watch ABC's *American Bandstand* and its host and my idol, Dick Clark.

American Bandstand had become a way of life for most of us. I believed there wasn't a lonely teenager in all of America because of that show. It united us. It was as if we were all together at a giant rock and roll party. Besides, it was always happier in the house when "Bandstand" was on. With its 40 percent lions share rating, it was daytime TV's number one show ever. It literally changed the face of the American Pop Music scene and it was the sur-fire vehicle that catapulted unknowns from obscurity to superstardom almost overnight.

Mr. Clark's young Philadelphians, the kids who danced on the show, set the trends in everything: clothes, fads, slang dance, and music. If Carol decided to change the color of her hair, a lot of us thought maybe we should try it too. To me, Dick Clark was something of a deity. He was American personified – like the Lincoln Memorial or Philly's Liberty Bell. In vicarious rapture, I gazed as Justine and Bob slow danced while Sam Cooke expressed their sentiments with "You Send Me". I danced along with little Peggy, trying to learn her newest steps as she tore it up "At the Top". I watched that attractive pair, Fran and Mike do a mean lindy to Jerry Lee's "Great Ball of Fire", and Arlene and Kenny lead "The Stroll" like real pros.

I heard Dick Clark mention something about a new girl singer, so what else is new, I thought. Another girl singer. There are ninety-five million females in the country and I'll bet ninety-five percent of them sing. "There is no doubt about it", predicted Mr. Clark. "She's headed straight for the number one spot".

I began feeling sorry for myself and a bit envious too. Good luck to her I thought. And then Mr. Clark just happened to play a song called "Whose Sorry Now?" My who's sorry now"? It was a total surprise, a complete shock. Well, the feeling was cosmic, just cosmic! The ruckus I raised was startling enough to tear thirty odd ravenous Italians away from their mountainous portions of Manicotti, and everybody knows that's no mean feat!

"Daddy! Mom! Hurry up"! I squealed, "Georgie! Aunt Marie! Quick, Dick Clark is playing "Who's Sorry Now?""

"Oh yeah? Someone else cut the thing too, huh"? Daddy said with his customary optimism.

"No, no Daddy! Listen! It's my "Who's Sorry Now?""

"Nah, can't be. It's been out too long. The thing's dead".

"Daddy, for God sake, will ya' listen already! Quiet."

We all have milestones in our lives, but more often than not, we recognize them only in retrospect. This milestone wasn't like that at all. I recognized it in five seconds flat. What I didn't know was that I would forever be able to pinpoint the precise moment that turned my life around-a sharp 180-degree turnaround.

Nineteen fifty-eight was a sweeter time, a more innocent time, not only for me, but for the entire country. Our teenage world was a world of pajama parties, diaries with keys, friendship rings, and who got pinned. A writhing Elvis begged, "Wear My Ring Around Your Neck", and we yearned to oblige the boy. When he was drafted into the army and his famous locks were shorn military-style, we mourned the passing of those locks. Each hair was probably worth a hundred dollars on the open market. Our pin curls were replaced by rollers, our bobby socks by colored tights. We wore pedal pushers, the sack, strapless prom dresses, teased hairdos, and the pageboy cut. Fifty-eight was a year of significant firsts: we saw our first transistor radio, our first jet plane, and our first stereo hi-fi player.

The country went fad-crazy that year too. We swiveled our hoola hoops and made stars of every male group smart enough to sing a lot of "Doo-wah, doo-wahs". College students swallowed their goldfish and crammed themselves into phone booths.

Even the records we bought had a gimmick. Alvin and his Chipmunks sounded like an LP played at 45 rpm; the sounds of "The Witch Doctor" pounded at our senses; and Sheb Wooley warned us of those horrific "Purple People Eaters." We bought 'em all, from "Ally Oop" and "Yakkety Yak" to "Short Shorts" and "Itsy-Bitsy Teeny-Weeny Yellow Polka Dot Bikini." The bikinis were teeny-weeny as a girl singer's chances for success those days. For several years now, no major female recording artist had surfaced; it was a totally make-dominated market. Small wonder that I was so flabbergasted that day.

"Will somebody pinch me please"! I shouted to a captive but enthusiastic audience. "Okay, family members, all those seeking my autograph, line up to the right. I may not wanna hang with you guys anymore. I'm a star, you know"! I'll make you see stars, warned Ida, bringing me down from my lofty cloud as if I'd hit an air pocket. "Well, what did I tell ya'?" daddy said, reveling in sublime and supreme satisfaction. And so he should have. He was the one who insisted I record that old song, written in 1923 and known to just a handful. Not any more!

Ava Gardner

Ava Gardner

My Story
By Ava Gardner
Bantam Books, 1990

I Only Did It for the Money, Honey!

As far as my career as an actress went, *Mogambo* was probably as close to a pinnacle as anything I've done. I did get nominated for an Academy Award for best actress though I was more relieved than upset when the Oscar went to Audrey Hepburn in *Roman Holiday* and I was told that I came within one vote of winning the New York Film Critics award, with even Bosley Crowther of the *Time* magazine, who usually treated me like a bad smell, fighting gallantly in my defense.

If you sense a little ambivalence in my thoughts about my ability as an actress, you're right. On one level, all I wanted to be was an actress, and I often felt that if only I could act, everything about my life and career would have been different. But I was never an actress – none of us kids at MGM were. We were just good to look at. Making things worse was that I really didn't have the correct emotional makeup for acting. If I'd had more drive, more interest, maybe I could have done better, but I disliked the exhibitionistic aspects of the business and the work was terribly frightening to me.

My mouth would always dry up so completely when I was on the set that I had to keep lemon juice handy and take a sip from time to time. I remember a cutter once saying, "I'd like you to see what I have to take out of your scenes." He ran them through for me and there were all these audible clicks where my mouth had gone dry." I'm afraid there are two or three places where I just can't get the clicks out", we'll have to redub." I told him that even in redubbing I'd need a drop of scotch or the clicks would still be there.

Given all this, why did I keep doing it? The answer I usually gave was, "for the loot, honey, always for the loot," and there was more truth than poetry in that remark. I had to do something, and I didn't know how to do anything else. I once thought about becoming a nurse, but I knew I'd vomit every time a patient vomited, and I wouldn't be much use. I could have been a secretary again, brushed up on my Atlantic Christian College dictation speed of a hundred and twenty words per minute. But I knew that would make me really crazy.

The truth is that the only time I'm happy is when I'm doing absolutely nothing. I don't understand people who like to work and talk about it like it was some sort of goddamn duty. Doing nothing feels like floating on warm water to me. Delightful, perfect. Maybe I just didn't have the temperament for stardom. I'll never forget seeing Bette Davis at the Hilton in Madrid during my promotional tour for *The Barefoot Contessa* in 1953. I went up to her and said, "Ms. Davis, I'm Ava Gardner and I'm a great fan of yours." And do you know, she behaved exactly as I wanted to behave. "Of course, you are my dear," she replied, "of course you are." And she swept on. Now that's a star.

Whoopi Goldberg

Whoopi Goldberg

The Whoopi Goldberg Book
By Whoopi Goldberg
William Morrow, 1997

Let's Talk About Farts

We all fart, right? We all get that cramp that tells us there's an air bubble percolating in our butt and it needs to escape. But we don't like to talk about it. Everybody does it and no one talks about it. Why is that?Let's break this down. Let's consider the fart in all its wonder. The public fart is a very tricky thing. It's all tied up in where you are, and who you are, and who you're with and what you ate for lunch. Most people, when they feel a fart coming on, they get up and make for the door, because they're not always sure what that little cramp is telling them. It could be a fart, or it could be one of those power dumps disguised as a fart. You go to let the air out a little bit and you're surprised by the actual materials you've deposited in your pants. Public farts are troubling enough, but these surprise power dumps are especially upsetting.

For the most part, a fart is just a fart. We feel it coming. We know what it is. And we usually have enough butt control to drop 'em at will or hold 'em back for a more appropriate time, or ease 'em out slow and silent. The game is in figuring out which approach to take, and then what to do with yourself after you've made your deposit.

I'm a great believer in claiming farts. Always have, always will. I don't want to be blamed for one of yours. Mine I know. Mine I can control. Yours, who the fuck knows what's going on down there?

Fart strategy can be tricky. If you're at a party, or a meeting, and you have to drop a little biscuit, do you drop and sit or do you drop and cross the room? Does the smell go with you, or does it stay behind? To the best of my figuring, you're nailed either way, so it's probably better to stay where you are and let the seat cushions absorb the brunt of it. If you move around, you take it with you, and it's just like leaving another one far on the other side of the room. There's no sense compounding the problem with a second had fart. If you're too chicken shit to cop to it, don't get up. Wait it out. And remember, just because you're sitting on it doesn't mean it's not gonna shake its way up and around you. Its gas, and it will come up through your thighs, and people are gonna know it's you anyway. But if you just keep on talking, then suddenly stop and look around to see where that mystery smell came from, that could add to the effect.

The theatrical stage gives a great perspective on farts and farting. You look out across those lights and you can just see the farts on people's faces. The smells don't always find you, all the way up on the stage, but those facial expressions make it plain. In a Broadway house, a lot of the people hurry through a pre-theater dinner to make the curtain, and they all bring their farts with them. You'll seem someone's eyes pop out, really big, like in one of Rodney Dangerfield's double takes. Or you'll see people squirming in their seats all crinkled up, like they're trying to hold something back. And then you'll see the people looking around in desperation. They've got their noses pointed up, scoping out some clean air. And you can almost see the gas float from one row to row to the next, like in a Pepe Le Pew cartoon. The people just fall like dominoes. I always look for the person who's sitting up straight, pretending he doesn't smell anything. He's almost always the culprit, because the key to dropping a fart is you have to smell it too. You have to look as indignant as everyone else. You can't protest too much, in case they trace it back to you, but you've got to protest a little. You've got to go through the motions.

Among the cast and crew, there's a whole farting convention. When I was in *A Funny Thing Happened on the Way to the Forum* on Broadway, there was all kinds of running around in the show, so a lot of times the fartee discovered the fart before the farter was even aware of it. When you're moving around like that, you don't always realize you leave a little trail. Stuff happens. You leave it so people run through your farts when they're crossing the stage. It's like hitting a wall, and they're breathing hard so they've already inhaled it. It's in their lungs, they know it and they know it's too late to do anything about it.

That's why actors are fucked up.

Chelsea Handler

Chelsea Handler

My Horizontal Life
By Chelsea Handler
Bloomsbury USA, 2005

Look Who's Having Sex with Mommy

I was seven years old when my 13-year-old sister Sloane, told me she'd give me five dollars to run upstairs into my parent's bedroom and take a photograph of them when they were having sex. At that age I had heard of sex, but I had no idea what it looked like. There were many nights when me and my five siblings would hear loud bumping and raucous laughter coming from their bedroom. My brothers and sisters always reacted with disgust and, being the youngest, I would follow suit but was never sure why. Without knowing exactly what the act of sex entailed, there wasn't any real reason to be revolted, but it had become second nature to me to pretend I knew something I didn't.

And besides, I was always up for a chance to make easy money. I had been wearing hand-me-downs since I was born, and by the age of seven I was already tired of my second-string wardrobe. I may not have known what sex was, but I did know that I needed to step up my appearance in order to be taken seriously in my forthcoming entrance to the first grade. "No problem," I said. "Where's the camera and how do I use it?" I tiptoed up the stairs leading to my parent's bedroom with Sloane following close behind. The door had a lock on it, but it was old and didn't secure inside the door jamb anymore. It just needed a little physical force to open it and on a 1-2-3- count Sloane asked "ready?" I nodded. "Then go," she whispered.

Now I know it's been said that seeing one's parents naked is not something you easily recover from. Now I know it's perfectly true. What I saw was reason to put myself up for adoption. My mom then jumped off the bed naked except for a nurse's hat on and dad was totally naked too except for a red bandanna around his neck. Fortunately, I took the first photo before the horror had a chance to register. The second photo was of my father's torso heading toward me with a belt. My sister led the rush all the way down to the basement laundry room with me close behind. We dove into a pile of dirty clothes and covered ourselves up beneath them. Then I realized that I had to get up and lock the laundry room door, which thankfully worked just fine. Dad demanded we open it and launched into his standard "I'm counting to three" routine. My sister, after just "two!" was ready to surrender but not me. "Open the damn door, now!" dad demanded. "three!" We were afraid he'd actually break it down but then he'd have to fix it, so it seemed we might be able to wait it out.

"I heard men fall asleep after sex," Sloane whispered. But dad didn't seem sleepy to me. He kept pounding the door and giving direct orders. "We have to get up and just let him hit us, "my sister said as she began to shake and whimper. I tried to comfort her by rubbing her back like my mother would do but I admit I was also too preoccupied with my imminent spanking to be very reassuring. "I just want to get it over with," she replied. "No fucking way! I am not going out there to be smacked!" This was the very first time I said "fucking" in front of anyone and I liked the way it sounded. I had heard my brothers and sisters saying it but never previously dared to say it myself. Instead, I would practice saying it alone in my room, lots of times. "Fucking this" and fucking that." My favorite was, "What a fucking cocksucker!"

The plan was to say this casually to one of my new friends in the first grade, while one of our teachers just happened to be walking by. No one in kindergarten ever really got my nascent sense of humor, so I was determined on making my mark in the first grade. We waited for what seemed like hours but was probably no more than five minutes. My father appeared to have tired out after all. Then Sloane said, in her whining way, "I'm hungry. I wonder where mom is?" With that she slowly got up and placed her ear by the door, No sound. "I think the coast is clear," she said. I was not sure. Then, cautiously, she unlocked the door. Again, no sound of an enraged father. She opened the door, stuck her head out and gave me a final, wistful look as she excited the laundry room. For a few seconds I thought she had made it but then I heard a definite slap across the face and a scream of torment. My next thought was how she would look eating a peanut butter and jelly sandwich with a fat lip. Maybe I can get out of my punishment by doing the laundry, I thought. Mom might even come to my defense. But I hate doing laundry, so I scratched that idea. I'll just wait it out and stay down here. I can pee in the laundry tub. Dad will be cooled down by morning. And so, sleep I did, but I was full of regrets for missing *The Cosby Show*.

Morning came. Sloan looked at me like I was criminal, or I enjoyed a bowl of Lucky Charms. I felt more and more confident as the morning progressed. The other kids were in awe of my nonchalance but not one of them mentioned the incident of the night before. We all braced for danger when dad came into the kitchen. He seemed to be his old amiable self. Mom, on the other hand, was nowhere to be seen. I felt victorious even if the film in the camera was sitting in the garbage can. All I could think about was how I was going to tell all my new first grade friends how I saw my parents having sex. But I would never admit I still didn't know exactly what it was.

Goldie Hawn

Goldie Hawn

A Lotus Grows in the Mud
by Goldie Hawn with Wendy Holden
G.P. Putnam's Sons, 2005

In Deepest India

Welcome to India. "What is the purpose of your trip here?" the immigration official asked me at Delhi International Airport. "Work." "And what would you be working on?" "Oh, are you going to Bollywood?" "No." Actually it's an English documentary. "And how long will you be staying?" "Oh, I don't know, two weeks." He nods and stamps my passport. As I gather up my papers, he asks, what is the subject of your documentary? "It's about the Asian elephant. I'm highlighting its plight and doing what I can to save it." "Very Good."

Touching a small statue of Ganesh, the Hindu elephant god, which sits on his desk, he says. "This will bring good karma." I walked out of the airport into the middle of a sultry Indian afternoon. I'm immediately hit by a wall of heat, the pungent smells of cooking and burning, the crush of humanity welcoming me back to a place my soul calls home.

At my hotel, I meet up with the rest of the team from Tigress Productions. My new troupe of traveling documentarians. Dizzy with jet lag, I have a quick dinner with the crew, who are all fabulous and fun and full of life. As we all retire to our rooms for sleep, the director, a lovely English gentleman named Andrew Jackson, advised us to eat a hearty breakfast before we leave tomorrow. It sounds a bit ominous to me. I wonder what he has in store for us.

In bed, I lie awake for a while, too jet-lagged to sleep. This is my first documentary. I'm happy to be documenting my personal story to find "my" elephant, Belly Button, a blind mother I first set eyes on seven years before on a game reserve deep in the south of this amazing country. Wonder if I'll find her. I closed my eyes and counted elephants. The next day, we flew to Nagpur, in the heart of India for the start of our journey to our first port of call, Kipling Camp. I am greeted by my new driver and much to my chagrin, I am led to yet another old Ambassador, a Jeep-like vehicle. How long is this drive? I asked. "Five and a half hours," he answers. I now understand why we needed to eat a big breakfast. I'm glad I did. I've been in these cars before you know, and they nearly always break down." He nods and smiles but nonetheless carries on organizing our convoy of six Ambassadors, dividing us all up with our luggage into separate car as is the custom and for comfort's sake. Game for anything, I climbed in my car and off we set on our caravan, honking horns and waving cheerful good-byes. After my hearty breakfast, all I have with me is some bottled water, a packet of crackers and a tiny jar of peanut butter.

Setting off, I'm quickly reminded of the exhilarating chaos of driving in India, swerving left and right to avoid rickshaws, children, street beggars and sacred cows. There elephants, and giant Tata trucks, their cabs adorned with effigies of gods, tinkling bells and vibrant garlands of marigolds all the while belching vile black exhaust. Out my windows I see stalls selling great pots of spices: saffron, cumin and turmeric. I peer into shops cascading with the most exquisite silks. I watched women in gaily colored saris walking down the street with children on their hips and baskets on their heads. Trying to keep up with the convoy, we chug, chug, and chug past trucks and slow-moving oxen, lucky to reach a speed of thirty miles per hour, cars heading straight toward us all the while. I closed my eyes. With no shock absorbers, we bounced in and out of every pothole, which are more numerous than people. After just a short time, I felt like my gallbladder and liver had swapped places. Jumping and jolting around on the backseat of the car, here I am embarking on yet another harrowing road trip across this country that I love, taking my life in my hands.

"What in the world am I doing?" I laughed out loud, but after a few hours, I am not so happy. "How much further is it?" I say over my growling stomach. He smiles at me in the rearview mirror, his head bobbing on his shoulders like a chicken. "Not far."

The road becomes increasingly more rural, dirty and bumpy, with ever more potholes. If I thought I had no shocks on my first car, this second car is unbelievable. My gallbladder and my liver have now exchanged places again. By now, we're really out in the boonies. "Excuse me? Excuse me?" How far is it now? "I'm really getting hungry." The driver turns and smiles again. "Yes," he replies. Oh my God, he doesn't speak English! Not a good feeling when you're in the middle of nowhere. I'm horrified. Its pitch black, and I feel like I'm traveling down a narrow, bumpy road to nowhere. We just keep on going on and on into the darkness. I watched the other cars whiz past us. We're going much slower than the rest of them. "Excuse me?" I asked my driver, hopelessly trying to talk with my hands," Can you go faster, please, *faster*?"

Soon afterward, and to my enormous relief, he pulls the car over to the side of the road. "Are we here?" I asked hopefully looking around. But he simply gets out, pulls a mat from the trunk, kneels on it by a roadside mosque and begins to pray to Mecca. I feel like joining him at this point. Back on the road, we carry on driving for a least another two hours. I'm still starving, even after I polished off what is left of my peanut butter and crackers.

There isn't a drop of water left. There is no sign of our convoy and I have no idea where I am or where I'm going. I look at my watch: this journey has taken seven hours so far, with no end in sight. I keep thinking that just around the corner we will see a sign pointing to Kipling Camp, or at least find the rest of the group waiting for us by the side of the road. I secretly wish another one of their cars had broken down. Tapping the driver's shoulder, I tell him I have to use the bathroom. With much sign language, I eventually make him understand. Unfurling my stiff limbs awkwardly, I squat down in the moonless night. All I can hear around me are the sounds of the jungle. A few paces behind me, I hear a twig crack. Oh my God, a tiger could creep up and bite me on the ass? Please let me live to tell this story! I pull up my pants quickly and race back to my car in haste.

Back on the road, traveling at what seems a snail's pace, my driver is looking around furiously. My blood sugar is low, my body is exhausted from traveling and I'm losing my sense of fun and adventure. "My God, what if he is lost and doesn't know where we are?" I asked myself aloud. At that very moment, my driver stops the car, looks right and left in panic and does a U-turn. I knew it, he is lost. "Are we lost?" I asked, trying to stay in control. Is that what we are? He is not answering me. We are lost in the middle of frigging India? The cat in me is rising. Finally spotting lights in the distance, I throw myself over the front seat to at attract his attention. Pointing, I say, "lights, lights! There! Go down there!"

This looks right to me, and even if it isn't, at least there are people there. We turn down a long road and drive noisily and dustily into a clearing in which a huge open fire burns wildly, illuminating the faces of our distinguished English crew. Ah, there they are. I see them all gathered around the flames, happily eating platefuls of curry and rice, drinking beer, talking and having fun. Unfortunately, my blood is now boiling. Mark Shand, my elephant guru, who is a part of our team, opens my door to greet me. A tall man with a shock of blond hair, he stands there with a broad grin and dancing eyes.

"Welcome to Kipling Camp," he says in his impeccable English accent.

"Where have you been?"

Katharine Hepburn

Katherine Hepburn

Me: Stories of My Life
By Katharine Hepburn
Alfred A. Knopf, 1991

My Idea of Love

People have asked me what it was about Spencer Tracy that made me stay with him for nearly thirty years, during which we made nine pictures together, and this is somehow impossible for me to answer. I honestly don't know. I can only say that I could never have left him. He was there – I was his. I wanted him to be happy, safe, comfortable. I liked to wait upon him, to listen to him, to feel him, to talk to him. I tried very hard not to disturb him or irritate him, worry him, nag him. I struggled to change all the qualities about myself that he didn't like. Some of them which I thought were my best, I feared he found irksome. This was not easy for me because I was definitely a me, me, me person.

It seems to me that with Spence, I discovered what "I love you" really means. It means I put you and your interests and your desires ahead of my own because I love you. But we use this expression very carelessly. Love has nothing to do with what you are expecting to get – only with what you are willing to give – which is everything! What you will receive in return varies but it really has no connection with what you give. You give because you love and you cannot help but give. If you are very lucky, you may be loved in return. That is delicious but it does not necessarily happen. It implies total devotion. And total means all – encompassing all the good of you and yes, the bad of you.

Someone asked me when I fell for Spence. It was right away on our first picture together, *Women of the Year* in 1941. I found him irresistible, just exactly that, perfectly irresistible. I have no idea how Spence felt about me. I can only conclude that if he didn't like me he wouldn't have hung around. It's as simple as that and that's enough for me. He wouldn't talk about it and neither would I. We enjoyed twenty-seven years together in what was for me, absolute bliss. That's my idea of love.

Anna Kendrick

Anna Kendrick

Scrappy Little Nobody
By Anna Kendrick
Touchstone, 2016

I Steal the Toilet Paper

A press junket is a full day of interviews to promote one film. The film studio or distributor will rent out a suite in a posh hotel and schedule perhaps fifty journalists to talk to you, one after the other. Every first-time junketer will emerge from their room around meal time and say something like, "They're all asking the same questions. Can't we just give the answers one and ask them to share it?" The mistake there is the assumption that anyone is actually interested in the answers. This is not *Meet the Press*; no one is dying to hear about how I related to my character. I am only an actor, and they need hits for their websites. The key, I learned, is to do my part in an orderly fashion and go home. There I would secretly unpack the tissue and toilet paper I stole because I figured I didn't sleep in the bed, it was the least they could do for me.

At first I found junkets disturbing because I thought the journalists were purposely patronizing me. I've been sensitive to people talking down to me my whole life because I was always small and looked real young. When someone interviewed me like I was age twelve, I would get all huffy about it. Then, at my first Golden Globes

I overheard an actress being interviewed next to me and realized, they were treating Dame Helen Mirren in the same sugary, condescending tone. So now it is just as annoying, but I don't take it personally.

My junket tour for the movie *Up in the Air*, for which I was nominated for a best supporting actress Academy Award, was long and grueling. It started in Toronto and ended four months later in Tokyo. The press for the film was a beast because it was all so grave. As I didn't want to let anybody down, I tried to take it just as seriously. You can't imagine how soul-crushing it was for my misanthropic ass to be sincere for so long.

I felt like a fraud participating in a con. I was being flown around first-class, staying at hotels I could never afford and wearing clothes that someone else selected for me and I was petrified that I would be discovered as a basically dull human being rather than the ready-made ingénue I was expected to be.

Carole King

Carole King

A Natural Woman
By Carole King
Grand Central Publishing, 2012

Natural Women

The more my husband Gerry Goffin and I traveled back and forth between coasts, the less happy I became about being away from our daughters, so much. I decided we should look for new opportunities closer to our home in New Jersey. One of the most successful New York based record companies in the mid 1960's was Atlantic Records. Ahemet Ertegun and Jerry Wexler, who founded it about ten years before, had been diligent in looking for songs for its roster of R & B artists whose strength lag more in performing than writing.

One afternoon Gerry and I were walking down Broadway when a black limousine with darkened windows pulled up alongside us. The rear window motored down and revealed Jerry Wexler. He got right to the point. "I'm looking for a hit for Aretha." He didn't need to say her last name. Miss Franklin had already enjoyed several top hits and we knew she was a marvelous vocalist. We moved closer to the car to hear what else he had to say. "How about writing a song for her called "Natural Woman?" Gerry and I looked at each other and nodded, what a great title, we could do that. Wexler saw our faces and nodded back. We stepped back on to the sidewalk and watched the limo ease back into the flow of Broadway traffic.

"Oh my God, he wants us to write for Aretha Franklin!" I exclaimed.

"Yeah." I think I already got an idea," returned Gerry. With me bubbling over and Gerry thinking out loud, we continued to reaffirm our ability to deliver the requested song all the way to the lot where our car was parked. Arriving home, we put spent some time with the girls but since we were chomping on the proverbial bit, we kissed them good night and headed up to the red room, our writing den. I sat down at the piano and played a few chords. It was unbelievable how right they were, and we both knew it.

Four decades later, Gerry remembered it this way in a phone call as we reminisced about writing this song: "You sat down and out came some gospel chords in 6/8 tempo, which was exactly where I thought the song should go. You made it really easy for me to come up with lyrics. You made it effortless." I don't know that I would describe it as exactly effortless but our discussion in the car on the way home had been an important jumping off point. If Gerry thought my chords were exactly right. I was blown away by his lyrical imagery. As soul in the lost and found…a lover with a claim check. Even though he was my husband and song writing partner, I still was wondered how he came up with these ideas.

The very next day we recorded a piano-vocal–only demo and delivered it directly to Wexler. He listened one and said he loved it and that he'd get back to us after he played it to Ahmet and Aretha. We remained in limbo for days.

Most conversations between Gerry and I went something like this:

"Ya' think they'll like it?"

"Why wouldn't they?"

"Ya' think they're gonna do it?"

"God, I hope so!"

Days passed. We heard nothing until Wexler much to our surprise and delight, called to invite us to listen to the finished recording. Oh my God! Hearing Aretha's performance of "Natural Woman" for the first time caused me to experience a rare speechless moment. Few people would consider it hyperbole to describe Aretha's voice as one of the most expressive vocal instruments of the twentieth century. Hear that instrument touched me more than any recording of any song I had ever written. I knew that the music I had composed combined with the title and the words – captured the spirit of black-inspired gospel in a way that gave Aretha something familiar to run with and run she did.

In 1970, at the beginning of my own career as a performer, I recorded "Natural Woman" with a simple arrangement along the lines of the original demo. My version is slower than hers but has a few chords from producer Arif Mardin's brilliant arrangement. How do you follow Aretha Franklin? You don't. You can only precede her!

Eartha Kitt

Eartha Kitt

Confessions of a Sex Kitten
By Eartha Kitt
Barricade Books, 1989

The Day I Made the First Lady Cry

While I was staying in Washington DC in the summer of 1966 during my tour of *"The Owl and the Pussycat"* I was asked to speak to a community youth group called "Rebels with a Cause". These kids took me to areas in our nation's capital where the streets were unpaved and covered with mud and litter, looking like something from the horse and buggy era. Some houses lacked hot water and electricity and most had no inside sanitation. Jobless people were hanging about the tenement stoops and poverty was everywhere to be seen.

I was so moved by these kids' desire to improve their neighborhoods that I helped put them with local authorities and very quickly we got the attention of the press and city government officials. Hubert Humphrey, the vice president, heard my efforts and brought me to the attention of Lady Bird Johnson, who then invited me to The White House for a luncheon for fifty women activists. The question to be discussed at the event was this: Why is there so much juvenile delinquency in the streets of America? On the appointed day I was whisked to The White House in a limousine provided by the Secret Service. I was nervous as I walked through the doors of the north entrance, greeted as I was by a host of black faces with furrows of slavery still marking their brows. White gloved hands reached out to welcome me; the smiles on their faces showed a restrained kind of pride, at least we can come through the front door now. Many things went through my mind as I was ushered through the corridors, think of those who had been residents before. It made me shudder as I wondered how many of them thought of Indians, Blacks and women as being included in the Declaration of Independence, the Bill of Rights and the notion of laws of the people, by the people and for the people.

It was Hollywood time in Washington. The Razz-ma-tazz protocol atmosphere began to hit me as I was introduced to the other invites. I was the sole black guest that day but I still hoped it might become a constructive opportunity to air the problems we had supposedly gathered to talk about. Imagine my surprise and chagrin when I learned that the topic of discussion had been changed to Beautifying America. I was never given an explanation why this happened and I was severely disappointed. I didn't think clearing slums and building affordable housing was what they had in mind by beautification.

The president made a surprise entrance and told us to return to our communities to tell them what a great family we have in The White House. Then he made a brief speech to us fifty ladies that was so banal that I doubt anyone of us could remember it except of that initial statement, which hit my ears like a boomerang. But out of the nonsense of his remarks came something about making funds available through social security for seniors to do something or other at the age of something or other. I raised my hand to ask about the when of the something or other. I said that if parents had to hold down two or three jobs to make ends meet they had to leave their children in a latch-key situation or exist in a wandering world of risk and trouble.

What is the president's solution to this kind of problem? "Well, we are building a better social security system for older…" and his nonsensical words, drifted into more irrelevant nonsense before he was suddenly snatched away by his security people. He was obviously not prepared for such a question. Back through the Walls of Jericho he went, not to be seen again for the rest of the luncheon.

I don't remember the menu, I only remember the hue, the atmosphere, the hopes, the desires, the wishes and the excitement of the other forty-nine ladies at being hosted by the First Lady. But there we were, talking about beautifying the country instead of our at risk youth. As the discussion moved around the Blue Room, each lady named the area of her commitment after describing what and how her community involvement led to her being invited to The White House. The original issue was studiously avoided. I raised my hand often but was told by Mrs. Johnson that I would soon get my turn. I sat down and waited, getting more and more inpatient.

"I think we are missing something here today," I said when she finally gave me the floor. "I thought the topic we are here for is why there is so much juvenile delinquency on American streets." Heads began to dip into laps but I couldn't restrain myself now that I had the floor. I then went on to correct the problems of our nations' youth with feelings of hopelessness brought on by poverty, lack of supervision, drugs, crime and mass depression due to the dissolution of strong family bonds. I could hear sighs of disbelief as I continued along their line. Then I continued, saying my talks with kids all over the U.S. often focused on our involvement in Vietnam. It is a war without explanation. "I have a daughter," I said, "but if I had a son, believe me, I would do everything in my power to have him live by the Ten Commandments and the lesson of The Bible. Thou shall not kill, Thou shall not steal Do unto others as you would have others do into you, and so forth. Our children are snatched from us before they have a chance to know life, taught to kill, and if by chance the return, they are not retrained but simply thrown back into society. They are not given jobs, or even examined to see if they might have emotional or physical problems. They are not taken care of in any way. To beautify America, it seems, to me, is to beautify her with jobs and less taxes and getting out of Vietnam." Far off in one corner of the room a lady got up and said, "Miss Kitt, I'll have you know that I have eight sons and I would be honored to donate each one of them to the effort in Vietnam." I replied out of frustration: then I don't know what I can say to you, or what this luncheon is all about." And I sat down. "Just because there is a war going on," Mrs. Johnson said raising to her feet, "I see no reason to be uncivilized."

The luncheon was suddenly over. I could feel a sensation of discomfort coming over me, a feeling of overwhelming ostracization. I believe I had said what many others felt but were afraid to ay. But the truth behind our children's problems was not to be told not on that day at least. We were invited to show our support for the Johnson's for whatever they wanted to do. Be against them and you're out of favor.

The manifestation of what I had done was now perfectly absurd to me. There was no outbound limousine for Eartha Kitt. At the security gate I hailed a taxi that drove me back to my hotel where some of the representatives of Rebels with a Cause were waiting for me. Over the car radio I heard, "Eartha Kitt makes First Lady cry…" I was stunned,

"What did he just say?"

When I was greeted by the Rebels I was cheered and hugged. They took me to a community center where a party celebrating the results of my efforts on their behalf was in full swing. When I walked in, all quietly paid homage to my presence, which scared me a bit because I was still ignorant of the impact of my words at the luncheon. I remember in particular the remarks of a Black Panther activist. He congratulated me for telling it like it is. "You said the truth, the truth of what we all want to say to the mat at the right time in the right place. You had the chance, you took it, and you did it all for us."

I felt big and small at the same time. I had only said what came to me naturally – nothing had been planned – but I had seen the suffering of too many people all over my country, and having gone through this myself, I could not hold back because of protocol. I spoke to my mother-in-law's sister who was babysitting my daughter. I told her I had missed my return flight to L.A. due to the all-nighter I enjoyed with Rebels and their friends. I deliberately failed to mention my passionate debates with my Black Panther friend. "Get on the very next plane" Eartha. "Don't talk to anyone, don't see anyone. Keep your mouth shut and get out of Washington as fast as you can!" "What's wrong, Evelyn?" I asked. "Don't talk! Come home immediately. Get out of there now!" Evelyn screamed.

I could not imagine what she was so excited about. But I called and discovered that the next flight I could book was at seven the next morning. The Black Panther and I debated all through the night. "We must use violence against violence," he argued. "Violence only feeds on itself and makes us seek an endless cycle of revenge, I countered. Early that morning our heated discussion continued as he kindly drove me to the airport. I boarded the plane, sank into my seat and quickly fell into a deep sleep. I awoke at the sound of the person, "Miss Kitt, we've arrived in Los Angeles. But you should be warned there are an awful lot of reporters and camera crews clamoring to meet you." I was still groggy and lacked comprehension. "Here," he said, "you might need these." That's when he handed me a pair of dark glasses.

Gladys Knight

Gladys Knight

Between Each Line of Pain and Glory
By Gladys Knight
Hyperion, 1997

I Remember Motown

Berry Gordy *was* Motown Records and he ran it with an iron hand. In the early years, Motown was run like the old company store in cotton country. You got a salary but they docked you for expenses. For young artists, many of whom come from extreme poverty, the system seemed like a dream. Motown bought their artist cars, houses, and often even their groceries, but those expenses were always charged against their future earnings.

In 1966, Gladys Knight and the Pips signed a seven-year contract with Motown, which was longer than anything we signed with the five other record companies that had represented us to that point. We were put on salary like everybody else but unlike them, we kept close track of every penny. There has been a great deal written over the years about Motown artists who felt ripped off but our experience was fairly unique. As a veteran group, we knew a thing or two about the financial end of business, and what we didn't know, we hired our own lawyers and accountants to tell us. The others were naïve, unexperienced and too trusting and it hurt them dearly.

We quickly earned a reputation for being more independent than most Motown groups, which was fine with us. Berry kept telling us how much he loved our group and our sound and how much he respected what we had accomplished our own. We told him we wanted his input and his full attention to promoting us and our records. There was no doubt that he was a star maker. If he focused on you and your career as he had with The Supremes, the Miracles, Martha and the Vandellas, The Four Tops and The Temptations, you got songs, you got records, you got the press and the tours and the money.

We got a glimpse of life on the A-list at Motown, when we were sent out on tour with The Supremes in 1967. They were the headliners, we were the opening act. If it was intended to be a lesson in humility, it failed. We showed The Supremes a few things on that tour, and we were also exposed to a whole new audience thanks to their drawing power. We had known The Supremes for a few years. The first time we performed with them, we weren't yet with Motown and they weren't headliners. Back then they were just three young city girls, Diane Ross, Mary Wilson, and Florence Ballard from Detroit's Brewster housing projects who were struggling to get Berry's attention.

On that Motown tour, I shared a dressing room with all three of them. I could see how Diana already considered herself to be above them as a performer. Her reputation as a diva was richly earned from an early age. In fact, Diane's attitude and behavior earned her the nickname Miss Cute on the tour. She may not have been the most talented of the trio or, for that matter, the cutest, but she certainly was the most driven. When a performance did not click, I heard her fussing at Florence and Mary, telling them that they were to blame. Minutes later though, they emerged as The Supremes and Diana was back in character, giving a celebrity wave, showing that famous "stretch-limo" smile. By the time we met again on another Motown Revue, their official name had changed to Dianna Ross and the Supremes and they were one of the hottest acts in the country. But Diana was still as competitive and driven as ever. And even though Berry was married and a father, it was an open secret that Diana was his main squeeze. And she acted the part.

In 1969, we were headlining at the Regal Theater in Chicago when we first saw a young group out in Gary, Indiana, the Jackson 5. Their father Joe, had brought them to the theater hoping they could audition for a spot in the Regal' s talent show the next day. Joe said all of his children were talented musicians and five of his sons formed a group with five-year old Michael, a pint-sized James Brown clone, taking the lead singer role. He promised to bring them by and he later did as we were talking to Rev. Jesse Jackson outside our dressing room. Joe introduced us to Tito, Randy, Jermaine, Marlon, and little Michael and I thought they were a cute, polite, quiet-mannered, and hungry apparently because they were carrying identical brown paper lunch bags. Joe asked if we could get someone from Motown to come and check out their act. I got on the phone to our manager at Motown, "Look, I know I don't have a lot of clout with you all, but someone should come down and see Joe Jackson's kids here at the Regal. Berry should see them himself. They're called the Jackson 5."

Our manager listened, and he said he would get back to me, but he didn't. When I called later, he again said he'd get back to me. Again, he didn't call. Nobody from Motown showed up in response to my calls on behalf of Joe Jackson and his talented sons. It was another Motown artist, and another of its outsiders who finally got Berry to pay attention to the Jacksons. Bobby Taylor, a member of The Vancouvers caught the Jackson 5 a few months later, after they became a regular featured act at the Regal. He arranged for them to audition for Berry who promptly signed them to a contract.

Berry sent them out to Los Angeles for prerecording rehearsals at Motown west studios there. They did so well it was decided to give them a song that had been written for another Motown group -- ours. It was entitled "I Want You Back" and Berry had actually been considering giving it to Diana Ross because it had turned out to be such a good song. Instead, though, he let the Jackson 5 record it, and it became their first hit. To add insult to injury, when it became apparent that the Jackson 5 were going to be superstars, Berry decided that this discovery should be credited to another one of his superstars. So not only did I not get credit for spotting them, neither did Bobby Taylor. For years after that, Motown press releases said that the Jackson 5 had been discovered by none other than Miss Cute, Diana Ross.

Jennifer Lopez

Jennifer Lopez

True Love
by Jennifer Lopez
Celebra/Penguin, 2014

The Messy Parts

Anybody looking from the outside would have naturally thought my life was great. A wonderful family, successful career; I was on my second season as a judge on American Idol and my latest single "On the Floor" had climbed to # 1 on the charts all over the world. What people couldn't imagine was despite these outward expressions of happiness, my life wasn't really that good or fun. My relationship with Marc, my husband of seven years and the loving father of my twins, was falling apart and I was terrified of admitting it to myself and others. Having had two previous divorces and the widely reported broken engagement to Ben Affleck the last thing I wanted to experience was the public fallout by another big relationship failure. The day the new of our split was announced was my hardest day ever!

But I refused to allow myself to feel like "a victim" even thou to do so would have been quite easy and quite an easy story to sell to the insatiable media monsters who pry and prowl my every move. The next year on my *Dance Again* tour, I deliberately chose to perform a song called "Que Hicete?" which means "What Was Said" about the truth of abusive relationships. What I hoped to say was that abuse is not gender specific and it's never normal. The performance features two couples on stage. One was a man being abusive to the woman and the other was the woman being abusive to the man. That number helped me face my own truth, I've never gotten a black eye or busted lip but I've been in relationships where I have felt abused, mentally, emotionally and verbally. I know what it feels like for your soul to be diminished by the way your loved one is treating you. It took me years to figure out that in that kind of relationship, the intensity and the conflict are created by both people and both are responsible for perpetuating it because every day that you don't walk out that door, every day you except awful things about your lover and yourself is a day is day that you're saying it's okay. Looking back at that time, I would be easy to conclude this is really a sad story. But I don't feel that way – at least not anymore. Now I feel something completely different…pride. It's the messy parts of life that make us human so we should embrace them too – pat ourselves on the back for having survived them rather than being angry for having gotten into them in the first place.

Part of loving yourself is about forgiving yourself, which is something I've always struggled with. Being ambitious, being a perfectionist means I've spent a life time beating myself up for not being good enough or for messing something up. It took a long time but I finally figured out that I wouldn't possess half the instincts or insight I've had as a woman and/or an artist if not for those screw ups. I keep dancing. I may not be getting all the steps right yet, but I'm dancing my heart out every day.

Sophia Loren

Sophia Loren

Sophia Living and Loving: In Her Own Words
By Sophia Loren
William Morrow & Co., 1979

Cary Grant and I

My very first Hollywood movie was an epic tale of the Napoleonic conflict in Spain called "The Pride and the Passion" and my costars were Cary Grant and Frank Sinatra. It was the spring of 1957 and the production was long and arduous plagued with problems and delays. We were filming in remote locations in Spain and I got to know Cary and Frank quite well. Especially Cary. We liked each other from the very first, and in that hot idyllic setting, with all our idyllic time between takes, we were constantly in each other's company. And such wonderful company Cary was! I was fascinated by him and with his warmth, affection, intelligence and wonderful dry, mischievous sense of humor. I was still only 22 and I had never met a man remotely like him before. Nor had he met anyone like me despite the fact that he had dated hundreds of women and married three of them. And we fell in love.

But I was also in love with Carlo Ponti, the only other man I had ever known intimately. So I became confused. I had known Carlo since I was 15 and we'd been together since I was 19. But even so, Carlo was an enigma to me. He was still solidly entrenched in a loveless marriage and divorce in Italy at that time was essentially impossible. And I sympathized with him; it is not easy for a man to renounce his family, especially when their children are young. But my sympathy was intellectual, not visceral or jealous. In my heart I wanted him to discard everything for me. I did not want to be a mistress no matter how much he meant to e. My whole sense of being rebelled at this role. I wanted the legitimacy in marriage that I had been denied at birth. I could hear my mother's words, "Wait around for him and you'll wind up an old maid good for nothing but lighting candles." And now here was Cary Grant, *the Cary Grant*, ready to renounce everything for me. Wanting me with no strings attached.

With every passing day he said he was more and more sure that we belonged together, that he finally found in me a woman with whom he could totally relate, to whom he could commit himself and to hell with feeling vulnerable. And he talked to me about us getting married. I couldn't answer him. I felt only conflict and contradiction. But I told him I didn't dare make a decision, that I needed time and to go back to my own environment and to be able to make up my mind away from the magic of the romantic Spanish evenings we shared together. Besides, I was committed to do a film in Greece and Cary was due to start work on a film back in Los Angeles.

As fate would have it, sixteen months later Cary and I were signed to do a picture for Columbia called *Houseboat*. I was to play a runaway who becomes a nanny to his young children. Of course the story had us falling in love even thou his character was engaged to a prim and proper ingénue played by the very beautiful Martha Hyer. Naturally I was skeptical but not nearly as skeptical as Carlo.

From the start of our filming together, Cary sensed a change in me. We were not as easy going with each other and I know it was principally my fault.

Although we often had lunch together, and it was always enjoyable, I knew something had come out of me, and Cary who was bright and sensitive, realized it too, it was not pleasant for me. I still had not delineated my boundaries so that I spilled this way and that. All I had done was established my negative limits: I would not go on in such an awkward relationship with Carlo and I would not sacrifice my Italian heritage and make a permanent life in Hollywood with Cary. But what would I do? What should I do? These were the only two men I had ever had any interest in.

Toward the end of the production the situation was finally resolved by a totally unexpected event and I learned of it in Louella Parsons column in the *Los Angeles Times*. On the previous day, it said, two Mexican lawyers in Juarez had obtained a decree divorcing Carlo from his wife. Immediately afterward these same two lawyers, one acting for Carlo and the other for me, exchanged marriage vows for us in a proxy ceremony before the same judges. Of course I had never heard of such a thing but it said a valid marriage license had been issued and Sofia Scicolone of Pozzuoli was officially and finally married to Dr. Carlo Ponti of Milano. I was stunned, it was scarcely the wedding I had dreamed of. But it was legal and not a fabrication for a hotel register. Mr. and Mrs. Carlo Ponti we were. Carlo took the newspaper from me and read it for himself. He was as surprised as I was. Of course he had initiated the proceedings after I created our "crisis" but he had not expected anything so swift and so public. I wanted to share our moment of happiness, to call someone, shout with joy but we had no friends and there was really nobody to call, except Cary of course. That evening we celebrated alone with a candlelight dinner in our Hollywood bungalow. I was surprised to discover that my secretary had sprinkled rice on our bed.

When I reported to the movie set the following morning, one look at Cary told me he had read Louella's column too. "I hope you will be very happy Sophia," he said. Bravely he kissed my checks and that's all he ever said about it. But finishing the picture with him was very trying and upsetting. Our important scene remained to be filmed and ironically it was the marriage of our two characters. And it was precisely the kind of storybook wedding I had always dreamed of.

Jane Lynch

Jane Lynch

Happy Accidents
By Jane Lynch
Hyperion/Voice, 2011

My Bossy, Know-It-All Vibe

I have to say I don't know why I am so frequently cast in the role of an authority figure, since the core of these characters doesn't match. I don't have that kind of confidence. I certainly don't experience the level of delusional cockiness I can portray in a role. But authority is so often projected onto me in art and life. I first noticed how people listen to me early on in Alcoholics Anonymous, when people seemed to hang on my words. Back then, I felt even less confident, so the difference between how I was seen, and my inner reality was ample and unnerving. Sometimes I felt the expectation so intensely that I would start pretending to be over confident in my day – to- day life. Now that I have earned more than a bit of my own confidence, I still don't really understand why people see me as so self-assured.

This bossy "know-it-all" vibe I gave off became my calling card, and I created a little niche for myself. As far as I could see, no one else was competing with me for it. I began to find different colors with in it and was happy to use it. I would be cast as the emergency room physician, conveying grave concern or the crusading attorney or those totally fighting for the rights of the downtrodden. For comedy, I could do all sorts of over-the-top, self-important characters. I'd be the guru therapist offering ridiculous advice as if it were the obvious choice or the controlling and demeaning television director abusing my minions. I did these vacations over and over again. I was working all the time, and really, I'd do any such character for any such job. Enter that monster.

Enter that monster Sue Sylvester, the acid-spewing narcissism-redefining cheerleading coach on the Fox TV series *Glee*. I thank the comedy gods each day for putting us together. In the run of celebrity fun for the success of *Glee*, there have been some bizarre events that have really emphasized to me how bizarre fame can be. Foremost among these was my invitation to be replicated in wax as Sue Sylvester for Madame Tussaud's Hollywood Wax Museum.

My wife Lara, her daughter Hayden and I were driven in a black limo to the back door of the museum for a big unveiling ceremony. I had gone through the meticulous measuring session a few months before, using ancient tools that looked lie instruments of torture, they calculated every part of my face in relation to every other part. The matched the exact shade of my eye whites and photographed me from all angles as I was slowly spun around on a Lazy Susan for humans. They ushered us very quietly and solemnly into a meeting room where guests were already assembled for the event. Among them were lifelike wax figures of Morgan Freeman, Halle Berry and Tom Hanks, which completely freaked me out. For some reason everybody was speaking in hushed tones. When the museum representative requested gravely that "the family come this way please" and led us to a waiting area, it suddenly seemed to me we were at a funeral mine. This feeling would only intensify when I finally viewed the wax likeness of myself. All I could think was, "This is how I will look in a coffin when I am dead." Though I was admittedly grateful they made my ass look great, I was also glad my last will and testament specified cremation of my remains.

After a reception they led us back through the working areas for a little tour. Imagine my surprise when I witnessed two workmen carrying my disassembled likeness onto an elevator. One was lugging my red trunk-suited torso and the other was carrying my head like a basketball. And to think only minutes before, I wondered if there was anything stranger than standing next to your life size likeness. The answer is decidedly – Yes!

Camryn Manheim

Camryn Mannheim

Wake Up, I'm Fat
By Camryn Manheim
Broadway Books, 1999

Naked at the Beach

As I was rehearsing my one-women show, "Wake Up, I'm Fat", that summer I found myself back at my uncle's beach house on Fire Island, a place I know well and am comfortable visiting because my uncle loved guests, and the thought of a happy family enjoying his hospitality. Frankly, I was only too eager to oblige him as it sure beat my lower east side basement flat. Being ever self-conscious, I was convinced a person looked thinner with a good tan, so one morning I set out for the beach, bikini and all, to get that slenderizing bronze glow. On this morning, knowing my family would likely avoid the hot sun and remain beneath the shady elm trees in his yard, I ventured out to the beach area called "The Pines", where all the fabulous and chic Manhattan socialites sun themselves against the din of the ocean surf and reggae music. I was feeling a bit risqué because I knew my folks would never find me, and none of the macho men would pay a fat girl in a two-piece much mind. So, I let it hang out, both of them that is.

I had been there about half an hour with my lotion and spray bottle when suddenly, I heard my mother's distinctive laughter. I froze and wondered if she had seen me and was laughing at me. So, I quickly rolled over onto my stomach and remained still. She, my father, uncle and aunt walked past without noticing me. I remained in that position for about forty- five minutes without the courage to move or look up to see where they had gone. As a result, I received first-degree burns on my shoulders and back.

That's how deep my psychosis runs.

Audrey Meadows

Audrey Meadows

Love, Alice: My life as a Honeymooner
By Audrey Meadows
Crown Publishers, 1994

Big Jackie's Big Heart

Jackie Gleason's weight ranged between 180 and close to 280 lbs, which is the fella would say, is a far piece. Consequently, it necessitated significant haberdashery expenses. He built three identical wardrobes to accommodate the erratic rhythm of his appetite. Like many robust personalities, he had a love-hate relationship with food that was masking some underlying feelings that were deeply rooted in the psyche. Periodically, when Jackie felt swollen with idle calories, he would check himself into a hospital and go on a rigid diet. He said this was the only way he could force himself to stop eating. His diet doctor would put him on a fruit and vegetable regimen but if anything, he increased his normal smoking from five or six packs a day to whatever he could get between his lips in waking hours. One day a couple of writers from the show dropped in to visit only to find the nurse making an empty bed and the great one gone. "Where's Mr. Gleason?" the nurse asked. "Oh, he fell sick," she explained, "so he went home to recuperate."

Each time Jackie incarcerated himself in the hospital, his scenic designer, Art Zerol would supply and build a model Lionel train, set at his bedside for him to play with. Art had made a living designing elaborate Lionel train layouts and dioramas for department stores and Christmas displays all around the country. That's why Jackie admired him. They had nothing in common except their love of Lionel train sets, which I later heard, was since as boys from impoverished backgrounds, they were not able to enjoy them as kids. When Jackie would finally spring himself from his self-enforced dietary captivity, the train sets would always wind up at a "Boys Club" somewhere in his native New Jersey. That's exactly the kind of man Jackie Gleason was.

Bette Midler

Bette Midler

A View from A Broad
By Bette Midler
Simon & Schuster, 1980

I Adore Deceit

Oh, how I love to be interviewed: How I look forward to answering certain questions which have, since they've been asked so often, become like old friends, family even like expected company whenever any interviews show up. Oh, those old familiar questions, the ones that make me twitch with discomfort, irritation even with the déjà vu if it all, questions that occur to members of the Fourth Estate with such killing regularity that I have considered the possibility of a vast intrigue against me, a conspiracy to make the worst of my colorful and engaging wit. Now, don't get me wrong, I adore deceit and I don't give a damn about being misrepresented or misquoted but I will not be made to sound boring to the millions who are convinced I am, if not a clever as Jackie O, well certainly the next best thing.

The decline in the quality of my reported interviews, I am convinced, stems directly from the clack of challenging questions put to me. For example: Question: How did you get your start in show business? What the interviewers really mean is, what it like was to work in a steam room with all those fairies dressed only in towels? For some unfathomable reason, the thought of a straight woman entertaining an audience of homosexuals in a bath house is to every reporter I ever met, at once repulsive ad frustrating! I am certain that whatever I may accomplish in my life, the headline will read "Bette Dead: Began her career in gay baths."

Therefore, I will now say what I hope will be the final word on the subject. It was a great job and a great experience! I did not perform in the middle of a steam room but in the pool side café next to the steam room. And I always performed in costume. It's true that occasionally I did wear a towel. But on my head, with some bananas and cashews hanging from it, a part of my tribute to Carmen Miranda… and all the fruits and nuts of the world. The audience there treated me with more respect than I deserved, especially considering I was brand new at entertaining that many people, clothed or naked, for more than ten minutes at a time. My act, if you can call it an act was more like a mishmash of possibilities than the coherent, noble show I perform nowadays, I was able to take chances on that stage, I could not have taken anywhere else. Ironically, I was freed from my fears by people who at that time, were ruled by fear. For that I will always be very grateful.

And by the way, just for the record, I never laid my eyes on a single penis, even though I was always looking for them, very hard.

Rita Moreno

Rita Moreno

Rita Moreno: A Memoir
By Rita Moreno
Celebra, 2013

Losing My Virginity

I actually lost my virginity twice! How is that possible? It isn't unless you repress the first painful experience, which I evidently did for years. I was a teenager. The extent of my sex education was the book titled *Being Born,* accompanied by my mother's "Here Rosita, read this." As I look back at that quite progressive act for 1943, I find it astonishing. But there was no discussion to follow-up my reading assignment. All I could figure out was that the man is a farmer and the woman is a field and somehow he plants his seeds in her. And perhaps this lack of understanding was why I became the unwitting field for the man who forced himself on me.

I felt increasingly uncomfortable around this man – my first agent, and in my total naiveté', I could not decipher his amorous signals. Only much later would I learn how common it was for aspiring actresses to have sex to get a part. In fact at that time it was more or less expected. The actual act had the speed and intimacy of a vaccination. I never told my mother. I would have to acknowledge it happened, buck up, try to forget it and move on. That's when my selective amnesia set in, I suppose. Until now. There was no background checks or child-predator awareness in the business back then. Thank God there are today.

Michelle Obama

Michelle Obama

Becoming
By Michelle Obama
Crown, 2018

On Politics

Because people often ask, I'll say it here directly: I have no intention of running for office, ever. I've never been a fan of politics, and my experience over the last ten years has done little to change that. I continue to be put off by the nastiness—the tribal segregation of red and blue, this idea that we're supposed to choose one side and stick to it, unable to listen and compromise, or sometimes even to be civil. I do believe that at its best, politics can be a means for positive change, but this arena is just not for me.

Priscilla Presley

Priscilla Presley

Elvis and Me
By Priscilla Beaulieu Presley
G.P. Putnam's Sons, 1985

Guru Elvis

There is an old Southern belief that holds that a woman goes into a marriage thinking she can change her man, while a man wants his woman to stay the same as when he married her. I didn't want to change Elvis, but I did have the romantic delusion that once we were married, I could change our life-style.

For the first few days after the wedding, I thought my dream had come true. We divided our time between Graceland and the ranch, where Elvis and I had taken up residence in a large, three-bedroom trailer. It was typical of Elvis to choose the trailer over the quaint little house. He never lived in a trailer before and it intrigued him. The place was completely furnished, including a washer, dryer, and a modern kitchen. It turned out to be very romantic. I loved playing house. I personally washed all his clothes, along with the towels and sheets, and took pride in ironing his shirts and rolling up his socks the way my mother had taught me. Here was an opportunity to take care of him myself. No maids or housekeepers to pamper us. No large rooms to embrace the regular entourage. I got up early, put on a pot of coffee, and started his breakfast with a pound of bacon and three eggs, proudly presented it to him the moment he woke up. You see, if we were ever stranded somewhere alone, you know I can take care of you."

Although the rest of the group traveled with us, they respected our privacy as newlyweds and, for the most part, left alone. I understood Elvis need for the camaraderie his entourage provided, and I didn't want to take him away from the people he loved, especially now that were married. He had always criticized wives who tried to change the status quo. He told me about one wife, saying, "she doesn't like him to be around the boys so much. She's going to cause problems in the group." The last thing I wanted was for Elvis to think I'd be the kind of wife who'd come between her man and his friends. Back at Graceland I decided one evening to show off my cooking skills for everyone by making one of Elvis's favorite dishes, Lasagna. I invited the regulars, bragging to one and all about how well I prepared this Italian specialty. Despite my outward confidence, I must have made ten long distance calls to my mother in New Jersey, checking and rechecking on quantities and measurements. It was important for me to prove myself a success. Elvis closest friend and aide Joe Esposito, our resident Italian and a "gourmet chef," kidded me all week about how he bet that my lasagna wouldn't be as good as his. All that ribbing only made me more nervous. I kept thinking, what do I know about pasta and Italian sauce?

Finally, the night of the dinner came. Everyone was seated at the table, watching me expectantly. I tried to appear cool and confident as I brought out the fancily prepared platter and started cutting individual squares for my guests. I noticed that when I started slicing the Lasagna, it felt a little tough, but thinking I was holding a dull knife, I continued dishing it out while Elvis said grace. I sat down, smiled anxiously, and said, "please start". We all took a bite and – crunch. There was a look of shock on everyone's face. I looked at my plate and was mortified when I realized *I had forgotten to boil the pasta!*

Elvis began laughing, but when he saw I was about to cry, he turned to his plate and began eating, uncooked noodles and all. Taking their lead from him, everyone pretended to enjoy it and were generous with their compliments. That's friendship! That's empathy! Joe Esposito still laughs about it, frequently saying, "Cilla, I'm still waiting for the Lasagna recipe you promised me."

Robin Quivers

Robin Quivers

Quivers: A Life
By Robin Quivers
Regan Books/Harper Collins Publishers, 1995

The Tampon Ads

My mother did manage to give me other valuable advice, when I asked her if I could use tampons, she said "No," only married women can use them. She used to shudder when I bathed during my period. When I started to experience painful menstrual cramps, she claimed, "You see god is punishing you because you take baths that time of the month."

When I pointed out that they recommended swimming during your periods in the tampon, my mothered answered, "Well maybe they can but we don't." Consequently, with a mother like that, it is no wonder I grew up ashamed of my body and sexuality. When I got the job playing opposite Howard Stern, I knew there was truth to the adage, "Opposites attract."

Gilda Radner

Gilda Radner

It's Always Something
By Gilda Radner
Simon & Schuster, 1989

The Highs and Lows of Passing Gas

On October 3, 1988, I had my third cancer-related operation in three years, this time in a big hospital in New Your City with a top surgeon and a renowned gynecological oncologist in charge. They were able to repair the blockage. Biopsies and a saline wash revealed no evidence of tumor activity. I'd be able to eat again, at last.

When I came out of surgery, I had a nasogastric tube in my nose and a catheter in my crotch, an intravenous feeding tube in my port-a-cath and a peripheral intravenous line in my arm. I went from 114 pounds to 134 pounds in two days because I was retaining fluid. Every part of me was blown up, and I spent a very uncomfortable two weeks in my room enviously overlooking Central Park. Dr. Greenspan came to see me every day and my case my case was followed by what seemed like twenty-five residents and interns, who all looked to me as though they were still in high school. I couldn't have the tube removed from my nose until there were signs that my bowel was working. The indication, if you can believe it, would be that I could pass gas. After ten long days, lo and behold, I had gas! When I had a bowel movement, I called

Greenspan's office to tell him. He was out so the receptionist asked, "can I take a message?" I said, "This is Gilda Radner. Tell Dr. Greenspan my bowels moved." This reminded me of my most embarrassing moments:

When I was sixteen years old, my girlfriend and I had gone up north to her parent's cottage. Because we went to a girl's school, we didn't see boys that much. There were a bunch of cute boy neighbors, so we invited them over. We had beer and some food, pretzels, popcorn and stuff. We were all sitting around, and the girls were on one side and the boys was on the other. We were telling jokes and talking and laughing and I started to laugh and by accident, I passed gas. Everyone looked at me with suppressed horror. It was obvious where the noise had come from. I was devastated. I was a nightmare – here's one of my first times with boys and I do the most disgusting thing. What guy will ever like me? How can they even think of having a crush on me?

Now here it was twenty-five years later, and I had all these guys waiting for me to fart! Here's life coming around again. All these cute, handsome residents and I say, I passed gas today! And they are so happy about it. I had wanted to wrap this book up in a neat little package about a girl who is a comedienne from Detroit, becomes famous in New York, with all the world going her way, gets this horrible disease of cancer, is brave and fights it. Learning all the skills she needs to get through it, and then miraculously, things are neatly tied up and she gets well.

I wanted to be able to write on the book jacket: "Her triumph over cancer" or "she wins the fight for her life." I wanted a perfect ending, so I sat down to write the book with the ending in place before there even was an ending. Now I've learned, the hard way, that some poems don't rhyme, and some stories don't have happy endings.

Nancy Reagan

Nancy Reagan

My Turn: The Memoirs of Nancy Reagan
By Nancy Regan with William Novack
Random House, 1989

Raisa Gorbachev, My Friend?

Ronnie met Mikhail Gorbachev four times in his second term because in his first term the Soviet leaders kept dying. First there was LeonidBrezhnev's death in November 1982, then the death of Yuri Andropov inMay 1984, followed by the death of Konstantin Chernenko the followingMarch. I was with Ronnie and his summit delegations on three of the fourmeetings with Gorbachev. Geneva in 1985, Washington DC in 1987 and Moscow in 1988, and each time my relationship with Raisa Gorbachev became a major story, in part, this was because the negotiations were closed to the press, which left thousands of reporters with lots of time but very little to write about. The truth is that despite the number of articles about us, Raisa and I were only a minor footnote to great events.

Her husband's sudden rise to the top chair of the Soviet politburo musthave become as a shock to her since in Soviet society, there had never been a concept of "first lady." In fact, the only time anybody ever saw the wivesof previous leaders was at their funerals. So, Raisa had to make the leap from obscurity to international prominence overnight. However, until the Geneva summit, seven months after her husband leapt to power, I don't believe her name had ever been mentioned in the Soviet press.

If I was nervous about my first meeting with Raisa Gorbachev, and I was, she was probably even more nervous about meeting me. I didn't know what I would talk about with her but I soon discovered that I shouldn't have worried. From the moment, we met, she talked and talked and talked – so much that I could barely get a word in edgewise or otherwise. During about twenty different encounters with her on three different continents, my fundamental impression of Raisa was that she never stopped talking or lecturing and usually the subject was the same: the glories of thecommunist system and why it is superior to capitalism. Once or twice she even lectured me on the failings of the American political system. At ourthird meeting in Moscow in May 1988, I was prepared to discuss drug abuse with her because many first ladies around the world had adopted it as their special interest, but when I brought it up, she promptly dismissed the subject by assuring me that there was no drug problem in the Soviet Union. Oh, really?

But back at our first meeting in Geneva, she had invited me to tea at the Soviet mission to the U.N. There she was dressed severely in a black suit, a white blouse and a flaming red tie. I later learned that this was the standard uniform for a Soviet school teacher and she wore it because official photographs were to be taken there and these would be the only photos released to the Soviet media and shown back home. For all my differences with Raisa, I did not envy her one iota. I don't believe I can imagine the difficulties, the pressures she must have faced. Here is one simple example: when the Gorbachevs landed in Geneva, I noticed that they go off the plane together and in customary manner, she descended the stairs before him. But when they returned to Moscow, he disembarked from the main door without her and she left discreetly from a rear plane exit with the staff and luggage.

Joan Rivers

Joan Rivers

Diary of Mad Diva
By Joan Rivers
Berkley Books, 2014

That Red Carpet

*D*ear Diary: It's January 30th. I really dread the arrival of awards season. Now days, there are so many awards shows, the Golden Globes, the Emmys, the SAGs, the Tony's the Oscars, Peoples Choice, Spirit Awards, Image Awards. There are more ceremonies to honor actors than there are stretch marks on Pamela Anderson's mouth. But I don't watch to see who wins them. As a matter of fact, I don't give a shit who wins; I'm much more interested in who loses. I love to watch how the losers mask their reactions when somebody else's name is announced. In fact, I tingle all over; I imagine this must be what a person in desperate need of an organ transplant feels when they hear the good news of a multi-fatal car crash not three blocks from their hospital room.

Yes, The Red Carpet is a special place to me. In fact, it is where I spent most of my formative years, from age 37 to age 80. It's also a magical place. Where else can an everyday ordinary *hausfrau* like me meet rich and famous superstars fresh out of rehab and make fun of their stylists' choices? Where else can B-list actresses show off their borrowed jewelry or their latest cosmetic enhancement? And where else, other than

Bravo of course, can pseudo-talent has-beens parade around pretending that anyone knows or gives a shit who they really are?

As most of you know, working The Red Carpet is not new to me. My daughter Melissa and I have been on more of them than Bob Hope and Billy Crystal combined. What I like about them most however is that they give me the chance to be part of the phony excitement and contrived glamor without having to endure the tedious shows themselves. I'm a busy woman. My time is better spent writing insults, designing faux jewelry, or cruising Craig's List for an eighty-year old man with eighty million in the bank and only eighty hours to live.

Ginger Rogers

Ginger Rogers

Ginger
By Ginger Rogers
HarperCollins, 1991

Why Fred Astaire and I Never Kissed

Over the years, many myths were built up about my relationship with Fred Astaire. The general public was led to believe he was my Svengaliwho snapped his finger for little Trilby to obey. In their eyes I was his creation. But the truth is far different. When Fred and I were casttogether for the first time in 1932's *Flying Down to Rio*, it was only his second film and my twentieth. While our dancing movies had a special kind of magic and produced a unique enchantment, it was certainly not the be-all or end-all of my career.

And there were also rumors that Fred and I hated each other and suffered through our movies, with him always ranting and me always bursting into tears. What non-sense! We worked together beautifully; we had fun and it shows. True, we were never bosom buddies off the screen but because we were so good together on the screen, the public – fed by the Hollywood publicity and press machines – inevitably made something bigger out of our massive partnership even though we were married to other people.

I still believe that Fred's wife Phyllis was a powerful force on all aspects of his career though you would never suspect it to meet her. Demure and soft-spoken, she would always come on to our movie sets with her knitting and sit on the sidelines quietly clicking her needles. I found her presence disconcerting, especially during dialogue takes. Fred was uneasy at these times too but it was never apparent in his acting, such was his professionalism.

Despite all the films we made together or perhaps on account of them, she never warmed up to me and she surely didn't want her husband to either. Other than on the dance floor, Fred and rarely embraced in our films even though our character always fell in love with each other. Fred made excuses and said he couldn't stand mushy love scenes and felt like a fool kissing in front of a camera. Frankly I believe he was just indulging Phyllis. When a script was released to Fred, the two of them would huddle over it and then he'd march off to the producer's office with a dozen reasons why it would be better if the lovers never embraced. One exception was in 1936's *Swing Time*, where his character and mine hide behind a hotel room door and when it opened to reveal us, he has lipstick on his mouth. Did we kiss off-camera? No siree! A makeup artist actually painted a lip imprint of Fred's face. That's why there are no intimacies between us in the ten films we made together. Our romance was accomplished with our feet.

Diana Ross

Secrets of a Sparrow
By Diana Ross
Villard, 1993

Hitsville

I have a special place in my heart for the old house on Detroit's West Grand Boulevard that is known around the world as Hitsville. The Supremes, like all the other Motown groups, were convinced that our unique sound came from the way our voices bounced off its old walls, the ceilings and windows. We recorded in every, and I mean every, nook and cranny of that building: the hallways, the stairwells, and even in the bathroom. The main recording studio, called The Snakepit was actually a converted garage. We experimented in every way we could dream up. The hallway with the windows open created a different sound than with the windows closed. When we sang next to one of the holes in the wall, that changed the sound too. The producers, the engineers and the musicians were so inventive and created those amazing songs with what little they had. Believe me, there was nothing fancy about Hitsville back then.

Have you ever sung in the shower and thought how pure and interesting it sounded? There was a small toilet closet in the rear of the make-shift studio, behind the control room. Somebody discovered (you can imagine how) that it created a perfect echo chamber. When I started singing leads, an engineer decided to hang a microphone above the toilet bowl to augment my tones. I remember late one evening when we were doing take after take and my throat was weak and I was weary and wanting to go home, finding myself singing my heart out and trying not to focus on the sink in front of me, and thinking, "I guess show business isn't as glamorous as I thought it would be."

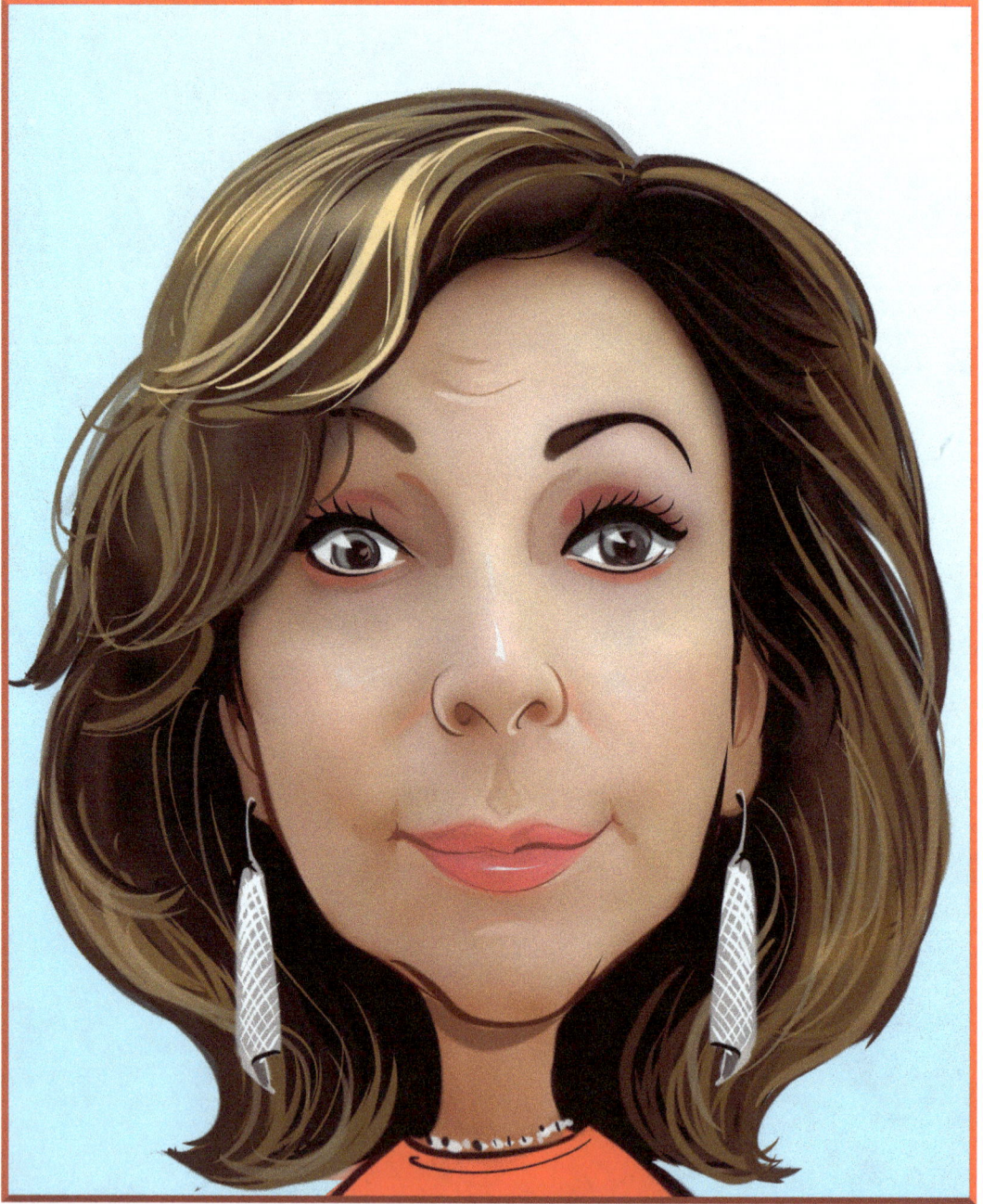

Rita Rudner

Rita Rudner

Naked Beneath My Clothes
By Rita Rudner
Penguin, 1992

The Art of Embellishment

I was a teenager pregnant, alcoholic, junkie, obsessive-compulsive hooker. Actually I wasn't. I just wanted to get your attention. You have just learned the first lesson of show business! Embellish. Make everything about yourself bigger, except your nose. Make that smaller and cuter, immediately. After you have made the commitment to embellish, hire a publicity agent to send out press releases that say you despise embellishment of any kind and that you would rather die than be involved in the act of embellishing. And make sure each press release is accompanied by a photograph and that each photo depicts you doing something absolutely proactive and wearing something absolutely revealing. When interviewed, say something controversial as this will assure prominent placement in the media.

If you find yourself unwilling or unable of lowering yourself thus, I would urge you to reconsider professions. But if you still wish to pursue a career in showbiz, be prepared to work extremely hard. Along with the frustrations, anxiety, humiliation and degradation, you may, at times, enjoy some success. And you may even, at times, enjoy yourself and have fun. And if you are really lucky, someday somewhere, some publisher may actually be interested in your points of view and pay you to write a book.

Take it from me, there are only two things you can do in showbiz and still maintain creative control. You can either write a memoir or have a baby. Both take about nine months and keep you up all night. The difference is books don't borrow money or marry somebody you disapprove of. At least that's what my publicity agent told me.

Monica Seles

Monica Seles

Monica: From Fear to Victory
By Monica Seles with Nancy Ann Richardson
HarperCollins, 1996

Grunting for a Living

The French tennis player Nathalie Tauziat was the first to use the press' obsession with my grunting against me. I'd played Nathalie in exhibitions and tournaments countless times. Not once had she complained about my grunting. We played against each other in the quarterfinals of Wimbledon. I took the first set easily, 6-1, and then we were tied, 3-3 in the second. In the middle of the match, Nathalie walked over to the chair umpire and said something to him. What's going on? I wondered. "Ms. Seles?" the umpire called. I walked over to his chair. "Ms. Tauziat is complaining about your noise". Hmmm, my noise. What was he talking about?

The following morning assorted tabloid headlines read: Seles grunts and players can't concentrate," "Seles almost defaulted." "Seles fined for grunting;" "we won't tolerate grunts at semifinals at Wimbledon." I tried not to care. It was the first time I reached the Wimbledon semifinals, and I was thrilled. I was scheduled to play Martina Navratilova. By then, Martina had won Wimbledon, a record nine times in her career. Facing her on the grass would be a challenge. Not only was she favored, but the crowd was strongly behind their champion.

I took the first set, 6-2. The games were closer and tougher than the score reflected. The second set was even more of a battle. We finally reached 6-6, which meant a tie-breaker against an equal player. Focus, Monica, I told myself as Martina' left-handed serves whizzed across the net. But moments later, not even I could keep my mind on the game. Martina left the baseline and went over to the umpire. I couldn't hear what she said, because the umpire covered his microphone. I was called over to the chair. "Ms. Seles, Ms., Navratilova has complained about your noise. Please tone it down", the umpire said. "Fine", I replied. "Just fine." I was completely unnerved and quick to anger. I walked back to the baseline. This is never going to end now, I thought with frustration. Martina won the tie-breaker, 7-3. We started the third set, and I felt my game slide back into place. That's when Martina went back over to the umpire. This time the microphone wasn't completely covered. I heard the words "grunting," and "pig" once again. I was called over and told to be quieter. I returned to the court and took the third set, 6-4 to win the match. I was going to play my first finals match at Wimbledon against Steffi Graf. Complaints or not, I was ecstatic.

Martina had lost, so she went to the press conference first. I went to the locker room and changed into a dry shirt so that I wouldn't get chilled. Then I walked up the steps to the conference. Martina was on her way down. "Monica, can I talk to you for a minute?" She asked. "Sure" I replied. I just want to apologize for what I said on the court. I was caught up in the heat of the moment. I know I can't take it back, but I'm sorry," Martina said quietly. At that point, I wasn't even certain what Martina had said to the umpire, because I couldn't hear her complain clearly. In a few minutes the press would tell me that she'd compared my grunting to a pig being cut in a butcher shop. Still, I wasn't upset with her. Martina didn't complain because she wanted to win by breaking my concentration. She was too good a player for that. I don't know for certain, but I believe that as she felt the game slipping, she began to focus on my grunting. Like a dripping faucet, it got to her. I appreciated her apology: she'd come to say sorry to me personally instead of sending a note through her agent.

The next morning the papers zeroed in on my grunting with this quote from Martina: "It just gets louder and louder. You cannot hear the ball being hit. I am not saying I lost because of her grunting. I would have said this if I won. I know she is not doing it on purpose, but she can sure stop it on purpose."

No one backed me up – not the other players, the press, or an official from the World Tennis Association. I was the number one player in the world, about to play in the finals at Wimbledon, and I was being attacked from all quarters. Commentators on television were discussing whether I should be fined or banned from tennis for my grunting. Tabloids were printing untrue stories. The upmarket newspapers were writing cruel articles and I knew I couldn't take much more, so I decided to change: I would hold my breath in after I hit the ball instead of exhaling with the force. When I stepped onto center court to play Steffi Graf in the Wimbledon finals, I only thought about one thing: don't grunt. It was one of the biggest mistakes I've ever made. Concentrating on something as stupid as grunting during a grand slam final – what was I thinking? The truth is that I wasn't. I was just reacting. Was it any surprise that I lost in straight sets? More than anything, I was disappointed in myself. No one had made me stop grunting for the finals: I'd made that decision myself. I'd been the one to fold under the pressure. I only have myself to blame.

Cybill Shepherd

Cybil Shepherd

Cybill Disobedience
By Cybill Shepherd
HarperCollins, 2000

When I Met Bill Clinton

*I*met our future president Bill Clinton in 1992, at a fundraiser in Los Angeles. This was during his campaign and his philandering was big in the news that week. I found him to be a very attractive and charismatic man. As his large right hand grasped mine, I whispered to him, "I better stand on the other side of the room. You don't need any more trouble."

Maria Shriver

Maria Shriver

***Ten Things I Wish I Had Known Before
I Went Out into the Real World***
By Maria Shriver
Warner Books, 2000

The Ten Things

1. First and foremost, pinpoint your passions.

2. No job is beneath you.

3. Who you work for and with is as important as what you do.

4. Your behavior has consequences.

5. Be willing and prepared to fail.

6. Superwoman is a myth and Superman is taking Viagra.

7. Children do change your career, and indeed, you entire life.

8. Marriage is a hell of a lot of hard work.

9. Don't expect anyone to support you financially.

10. Laughter really is the best medicine and time really does heal all wounds.

Sarah Silverman

Sarah Silverman

The Bedwetter: Stories of Courage, Redemption and Pee
By Sarah Silverman
HarperCollins, 2010

I Had Thought I Had Sex Before

I have never been raped. Let me rephrase: as I am writing this I have not up to this point ever been raped. But then again, in my youth, there were certain key incidents during which I was treated with such cruel and reckless abandon by the males involved that technically speaking, I probably have been around 10 to 12 percent raped.

Like in every girl's worst dream, my delicate flower was taken by a gruff thirty-year-old comic from Queens who is emotionally indifferent to me. His name is Kevin and he was the emcee at the Comedy Club in the West Village of Manhattan where I had a job passing out flyers. Besides my ten dollars an hour wage, I could go upon stage on open mike night without having to bring in two paying customers, which was otherwise required.

Kevin was tall with dark brown hair and a white and red blotchy Irish face. He wore a long green trench coat and carried a briefcase, which at nineteen, I found very impressive, and he was thirty, a grown man. One night he was standing outside the club smoking a cigarette. I went outside too and bummed one. As I hoped he started a conversation with me:

Kevin: So, you go to school?

Me: Yeah, NYU

Kevin: What – are you a freshman?

Me: Mm-hmm.

Kevin: What – are you like in a sorority?

Me: Yeah but you can only be in it if you are really cool.

Kevin: Yeah? How many others are in it?

Kevin: Yeah? How many others are in in?

Me: Only me.

He laughs. I got him.

I did my five minutes on stage and stayed for the rest of the night until the show was over and Kevin was ready to lock up and head home. "You wanna see my apartment?" He chuckled, I presume at this paper thinly veiled proposition, "Ah, it's in Queens."

"Sure," I said. "Yeah let's go."

And off we cabbed way out to Astoria. We walked up a stairwell and down a long hallway to his apartment door. Inside there was a small living room and kitchenette, two bedrooms, one his and the other his absent roommate's. On the coffee table was a cassette tape. *Best of Chicago* and a stack of record albums with the Go Go's on top. My kind of guy I thought.

"You wanna see my bedroom?"

"Okay."

He led me to his room which had a bed, a dresser an ashtray that desperately needed emptying. He then kissed me and laid me back in his bed.

"Have you ever had sex before?"

"Yes, I have had sex before," I ensured defensively.

Here's the thing: I thought I had had sex before. During senior year of high school, I visited my sister at Boston University and she arranged to fix me up with a friend who was from all accounts very good-looking. You know, the kind of guy who girls at school would think was really hot. He was in college; he was tall, lean and had long hair and a beard – like a sexy Jesus. We sat on my sister's tiny living room couch and watched a sexy, creepy thriller but fell asleep before anything really seriously between us happened. The next morning, with my sister and her roommate gone, we moved into the bedroom. He put a condom on and pushed against me, but quite honestly there was no hole there to penetrate. I figured that was it. The guy just pokes hard between your legs for a while. Sex. When he finally gave up, he said, "It's not like it is in the movies, Sarah, is it?" "No," I said, "it's not."

So, when Kevin asked me if I was a virgin, I answered honestly, no! But somehow, I think he knew better than me because he pretty much instructed me and directed me through the whole process. He talked me into my first blowjob (that I admit I had never done before); and through what to do with my lips and tongue, and what not to do with my teeth, and so on. And then, slowly at first, he pushed inside me. All the way inside me. And all I could think was, "Holy shit, THIS IS SEX. Dummy!"

Afterward, we had the traditional post – coital smoke. Then he put out his cigarette and pulled back the sheets to get up out of bed, revealing a large Rorschach – like pattern of blood. Like a red butterfly stamp, it got lighter and lighter with each imprint. There was a long moment of silence before I worked up the nerve to say,

"That came out of you?"

"Um, no it didn't."

Another long pause, this time broken by him. "It came out of you but it's okay, just buy me a new set of sheets."

Liz Smith

Liz Smith

Natural Blond
By Liz Smith
Hyperion, 2000

Remembering Poor Judith Exner

I guess I won't serve history if I fail to mention my connection with Judith Exner. When she finally died in 1999 of the cancer that had plagued her over the years, Judith's obituaries ran the gamut. The worst were in *The New York Times* and one by its columnist, William Safire, a man I admire and with whom I am friendly. Both described Judith derisively as a woman who "claimed" to have had a relationship with President John F. Kennedy. They seemed to take seriously the denials of Dave Powers and others that she had actually played an important role in negative aspects of Kennedy's administration. (I guess the *Times* doesn't believe the White House phone logs and the memos of J. Edgar Hoover and the FBI.)

Judith Exner was an impressionable, fun-loving girl from a good Los Angeles family. In her youth, she was said to have been more beautiful than Elizabeth Taylor. She fell in with a fast show biz crowd that brought her to the attention of Frank Sinatra. After a brief affair, they remained friends. Eventually she was in Las Vegas and Sinatra introduced her to the young, handsome Senator Kennedy, who was seeking the presidential nomination. Judith, a somewhat lapsed Catholic, says she tried to avoid involvement with the married J.F.K., but he pursued her relentlessly. She gave in and they began their affair. Judith fell madly in love. She claimed J.F.K. told her he and Jackie had an "arrangement" and would divorce if he lost the election. And after he was elected, she continued to see him but resisted J.F.K.'s gamesmanship. He wanted her to come to parties at the White House with Jackie present. She refused but went on believing that he loved her. That was before he met Marilyn Monroe.

Just before his election, Kennedy asked Judith to carry a bag of money to the mobster, Sam Giancana, in Chicago, but didn't tell her who Giancana was. Judith had already fleetingly met the mob boss via Sinatra, but says she didn't make the connection. She began to carry missives from J.F.K. to Giancana and set up several personal meetings between the president and the mobster. J.F.K. told her, "Sam's helping us to get rid of Castro." Judith claimed Bobby Kennedy was aware and complicit in all these activities. Many people believe that the original suitcase of money was actually used to help buy crucial Kennedy votes in the Chicago area. Judith claimed that by the time she realized who Giancana was, she had decided she liked him and felt he was her friend. She insisted to the end that she did not have "an affair" with him, as most people assume, and slept with him only once, after she and the president had broken up when she was in a despondent state.

Sam Giancana and his henchman Johnny Rosselli were both murdered after this. Marilyn Monroe was found dead in mysterious circumstances. Then both the Kennedy brothers were assassinated. Judith said she feared for her life in this aftermath and slept with a gun beneath her pillow. When a Congressional committee subpoenaed her to testify in 1975, she did so, reluctantly, feeling hounded by Congress, the FBI and the IRS.

Judith agreed to write a book of her life but opted out at midpoint and left her collaborator to, as she said, "mostly make up portions of it.". This book was Judith's downfall. It haunted her down the years and she had to perform several feats of revisionist history, which some skeptics still do not buy. She said to me plaintively, "I was twenty-five and in love. Was I supposed to have more judgment than the president of the United States?" Nevertheless, Judith gained the reputation of a mob moll, a party girl, an adulteress and a liar. Most people in those days didn't want to find fault in J.F.K. or Bobby, for anything.

Judith had gotten in touch with me after Congress itself had blown the whistle on her relationship with the president. She told them as little as possible, but once her spurious book came out, she found herself despised for having created the first crack in the Kennedy myth of Camelot. I liked Judith Exner when I first talked to her on the telephone in the late 70's. My internal shit-detector told me she was not a liar.

In 1996, I went to California and met Judith for the first time. She was a slightly plump but still beautiful version of the younger self, warm sweet and sincere, a woman whose life had been ruined by a forbidden romantic love and bad judgment. I then wrote for *Vanity Fair* what I hoped was the defining be-all and end-all on Judith Exner, including her last revelation-that after she and J.F.K. ended their affair, she had aborted his child in Chicago while under the care of the mob. Though the abortion or hospital stay was on the record, there was no way to prove that the child had been J.F.K.'s. I instinctively felt it was true. Most of Judith's other allegations, considered absurd at first, had panned out.

Judith Exner was a victim of her own beauty and innocent man-slaying sexuality. As a consequence, and despite the great men who romanced her, she is destined to wallow in obscurity. How paradoxical.

Suzanne Somers

Suzanne Sommers

After the Fall:
How I Picked Myself Up, Dusted Myself
off and Started All Over Again
By Suzanne Sommers
Crown, 1998

The Thighmaster

*D*uring the time I was speaking to groups about the unique problems children of alcoholics experience, which served as the founding purpose of the Suzanne Sommers Institute, which I co-founded following the publication of my first book, *Keeping Secrets* (in which I described the devastating effects on my emotional well-being caused by my father's drinking-induced rage upon our family) my husband and manager Alan said to me one night: "I've been thinking about our conversation in Las Vegas about passive income and I have an idea."

He had been routinely getting inquiries about me endorsing products and had rejected them all. Up to that point my only role in advertising had been in commercials for products like M & M's and Kellogg's cereal and others. "So far, nothing had really impressed me," he said, "but this guy who wants to meet you has a piece of exercise equipment and I think you could really make something of it.

You could inspire women by showing them that it is possible to stay in shape with minimum of effort."

"I don't want to do one of these exercise videos," I told him. "That's Jane Fonda Territory."

"Yes, he said, but this is a simple piece of equipment not a video."

That was the origin of the Thighmaster, a simple piece of exercise equipment that went on to sell millions of units and became a pop culture artifact in the early 1980's. How it came about is a good story that started with a visit to our home by the inventors of what he then called the V-Toner. It was designed to build and tone upper-body shoulders, arms, biceps, etc. I looked at it and studied it and practiced with it, then asked him, "Will this thing work for the inner thighs?"

"Oh sure," he said, "It's great for that area too."

Alan and I both continued to play with the V-Toner, looking at it from every angle. We decided that very day it should be renamed Thighmaster. In quick order we negotiated equal ownership with the inventor and his manufacturing partner. Our role was to handle the promotion. I admit I worried doing a fitness commercial might look cheesy, but Alan said, with his usual insight, "If it succeeds you'll be perceived as brilliant and if it fails no one will remember it."

Within the first week of our marketing campaign sales of Thighmaster skyrocketed. The 1-800 number sales center was operating 24-hours a day and big retailers like K-Mart and Target were displaying it prominently with life-size cardboard cut outs of me in my red leotard and Chrissy hair-knot. It became the number one Christmas gift for 1990. We were astonished, elated.

In short order I was booked on *Oprah*, *The Tonight Show* with *Jay Leno*, *The Late Show with David Letterman*, *Larry King CNN, show*, *Live with Regis and Kathie Lee* and others. We gave Thighmasters to everyone in the audiences of the Maury Povich and Jenny Jones shows. And I appeared on what seems like hundreds of local talk shows. The odd thing about it was that a demonstrated the product, I was actually getting my own exercise in. Talk about killing two birds with one stone! Then, Mel Gibson's production company called and asked us to use a clip of the commercial in his next movie, *Forever Young*. Universal Pictures licensed a different commercial in their remake of the *Nutty Professor* starring Eddie Murphy. Then Warner Bros. used it in their movie *Heat,* starring Robert DeNiro and Al Pacino. Even *Saturday Night Live* did a couple of skits parodying the success of Thighmaster. It also turned up in the storylines of sitcoms *Murphy Brown* and *Designing Women*. One day I turned on the television and watched America's number one talk show host, Phil Donahue wearing a Thighmaster on his head. But the topper was seeing the president of the United States George H.W. Bush on CNN speaking at the prestigious annual White House Correspondents Dinner. He said, in explaining why his spokesman Marlin Fitzwater was absent, that he had injured himself over-doing it on his Thighmaster. I screamed with laughter. CNN ran that piece over and over again. Later I heard that Thighmaster was an answer in the board game Trivial Pursuit to the question. "What is the biggest selling exercise equipment in history?"

"You wanted passive income, you got it!" Alan said, smiling from ear to ear.

Shirley Temple

Shirley Temple

Child Star
By Shirley Temple Black
McGraw-Hill Publishing, 1988

My First Kiss

Although mother and I discussed everything else, sex never entered our conversations. Fortunately, there was my closest friend, I'll call "smart girl" whose worldly mother had already explained everything pertinent. Another schoolmate produced a contraceptive device, an item secretly inspected with profound interest by all the young teen girls at Westlake School, a private academy I attended through the 10th grade.

By then graduated to a second-size brassiere, I was experimenting with my closet male friend Tommy Hotch. On a moon-drenched golf green at the Desert Inn in Palm Springs, we got hot and then we got cooled off when the automatic nighttime water sprinklers erupted all around us. The next day we warmed up again while riding a tandem bicycle. Reaching from behind, he fumbled one handed to undo my bra strap, taking far too long to allow me to show shock or even surprise. Despite Smart Girl's tutelage and my own experimentation, I was still not exactly sure what precise degree of intimacy produced pregnancy. After the Desert Inn petting sessions, my menstrual period was late. Such things were seen as a calamitous harbinger. Immediate action was necessary, but hardly a subject for consultation. Scouting mother's bathroom medicine chest, among her prescriptions for bladder infections and kidney stones, I found one pill bottle labeled "take as needed for delay". Extracting one tablet, I swallowed it, retreated into mother's room, and seated myself cross-legged before her full-length mirror like a monk about to perform a ritual.

What would happen? Would I become a werewolf? Grow a beard? I stared, my heart beating faster. Would I die? Nothing happen, of course. Nature soon verified that pregnancy was impossible in our cautious brand of necking, a discovery which encouraged Tommy and I to take up where we had left off. Naturally, mother know more of what was going on than we suspected. Accommodating the inevitably fickle will of her daughter, yet a stickler for propriety, she collaborated with Hotch to give me a what was then called a "fingerling," a tiny amber-colored diamond bracelet surrounded by sapphire-blue petals with a tiny dangling tag reading "forget-me-not". In retrospect, Hotch played his game with consummate restraint, leaving me chaste, if marginally wiser. He never was really imagined as a husband, any more than I as a wife. Our alliance was on the anvil, but never quite got forged.

Margaret Thatcher

Margaret Thatcher

The Downing Street Years
By Margaret Thatcher
HarperCollins, 1993

No. 10 as a Home

Number 10 Downing Street is more than an office: it is also intended to serve as the prime minister's residence. From previous visits during my tenure as Education Secretary, I knew that the building is much larger than it looks from the outside because it is in fact, two houses, one situated behind the other and joined by passages and a linking wing.

In some ways No.10 is an unusual sort of home in which to live. Portraits, busts and sculptures of one's predecessors remind one of the nearly 250 years of history into which one has stepped. As prime minister, I had the opportunity to make an impact on the style of No. 10. When I arrived it rather looked like a down-at-the-heel old fashioned gentlemen's Pall Mall club, with heavy and worn leather furniture and old thick crimson curtains. I changed the whole feel of the place by bringing in bookcases, tables and chairs from elsewhere in the building. Outside the living quarters I displayed by own collection of porcelain, which I had built up over many years. I also brought with me a powerful portrait of Winston Churchill from my chambers in the House of Commons. I had it hung in the antechamber of the

Cabinet Room so that it looked down upon all who gathered there. Over time I also commissioned significant redecorations, often at my own expense, and added many works of contemporary art as well.

I felt strongly that when foreign visitors came to Downing Street they should see something of Britain's cultural heritage. But when I realized most of the historical paintings were copies, I sought out originals from various museums and great houses. For example, I was lent a portrait of King George II, wo had actually gifted No. 10 to Sir Robert Walpole, our first prime minister around 1755. I also had some fine portraits hung of our nation's heroes and through them one can feel the continuity of our history.

I recall on one occasion watching French President Valery Giscard d'Estaing gazing at two portraits in the dining room — one of the young Admiral Horatio Nelson and the other of General Wellington. He remarked on the irony. I replied that it was no less ironic than that I should have to look at portraits of Napoleon on my visits to Paris. In retrospect, I can see that this was not quite parallel. Napoleon lost.

Marlo Thomas

Marlo Thomas

Growing Up Laughing
By Marlo Thomas
Hyperion, 2010

Daddy Being a Daddy

When I was growing up, my nickname was "Miss Independence," and it fit me well. I was clearly of the "I can do it myself" persuasion, and though my dad had warned me often that show business was very difficult-especially for women, I fervently-perhaps even naively-believed I could get where I wanted to go on my own. Still, the stories were legend, and quite scary, about how pretty young women were metaphorically eaten alive by ambitious and cunning studio executives, agents, producers and casting directors. Thus, my desire to become an actress became a long simmering sore point between my father and me. He had attended all my school plays and he always left worried. "She's got the bug Rosie," he'd would tell mom.

After two years of USC I was restless and told my parents I wanted to go to New York City to study acting. "Finish college first," said dad. "That way you'll always have something to fall back on." Typical advice for a man of the depression era. The day I graduated with a degree in elementary education, so I could one day become a teacher I let my parents believe, I handed him my diploma and said, "This is for you. Now I'm going to study acting."

A compromise was quickly reached. I could study acting and audition for theater as long as I remained in C.A., which dad reminded me, was far more promising for a young woman then dingy New York. I reluctantly acquiesced, for the time being that is. And so, I started plugging away at it. I studied, did workshops, appeared in plays, auditioned for every role I could, took meetings, mingled with show folk and knocked on every door I could find, and I was getting nowhere. Finally, dad couldn't take my frustration any longer and begged me to let him help me by setting up a meeting for me with a friend of his who just happened to be the head of production at Columbia Pictures.

Stubborn me felt like a sell-out but I went anyway. I sat across from the producer's large desk feeling both hopeful and humiliated. He began by telling me what a terrific dad I had, that he was a brilliant performer, a gentleman, and a great golfer. After a while I tried to bring the conversation around to me and my fledgling career, but he looked at me dismissively. "Why would a lovely, educated, well-raised girl like you want to be in this lousy cut-throat business?" Why don't you get married, settle down and give your father some grandkids?" You can imagine my anger. And even though dad denied putting him up to it, it was obvious to me they had more than a telepathic meeting of the minds about me. I was totally demoralized. I called my father and told him, "Don't ever, ever make any more calls for me again. I'm going to do this totally on my own!"

But as I continued to make my way, it continued to eat at my father that his daughter was pounding the pavement in vain. So, one night he decided to talk to me about it. Rather than try to encourage me and give me hope, he did his best to persuade me to abandon my acting career. He thought it was a long shot that lightning would strike twice in the same family and that I should rethink what I wanted to do with my life. The more he spoke the more upset I became. "You're an educated woman. You could become a senator for God's sake!" I couldn't believe what I was hearing. After all the years of unconditional love and support in everything I did growing up, he had withdrawn his belief in me. I was furious. "Not only am I going to make it," I screamed, "but someday you and your partners are going to want to hire me and you won't be able to fucking afford me! And I stormed out. Within a week I was in New York.

Later I learned that my mother overheard the whole thing and told dad to apologize to me. "Don't you think you were too tough on her?" she said. "No, let her be," daddy said. "If she really wants to succeed in showbiz, she'll have to learn to face a lot tougher rejection than this."

Tanya Tucker

Tanya Tucker

Nickel Dreams
By Tanya Tucker with Patsi Bale Cox
Hyperion, 1977

The Betty Ford Center

I arrived in Rancho Mirage and the Betty Ford Center and checked in late that night. It was a very nice place and certainly didn't look like a prison but I felt like jail was where I was headed. I knew that for the next thirty days, I'd be under supervision. Even though I knew I could leave at any time, I knew I wouldn't. Not after seeing my dad on his knees in fear. They checked me in, then searched my luggage for liquor and drugs, including nonprescription drugs. You can't even have most kinds of mouthwash because of the alcohol content. I ended up with three other women in a room they called the swamp, the room where Elizabeth Taylor had stayed when she was there. They explained that every room had a Granny, meaning the woman who'd been there the longest and that she was in charge of the day-to-day details connected with our living arrangements. I was told that my middle name Denise, is what I would be known as since they wanted no mention of my being a celebrity. Boy, they thought they didn't want it. Denise with last name was fine with me.

One of the staff members gave me a book about drug rehabilitation to study and a journal so I could write down my thoughts every day. I had some thoughts all right. I wrote down the name of every person who ever made me mad and exactly why they were rotten to the core. The journal was probably one of the few benefits I got from being there. Because it was the only place I opened-up.

Tina Turner

Tina Turner

My Love Story
By Tina Turner
Atria, 2019

Learning I Had a Learning Disability

... *t*here was a reason I had difficulty learning. It had something to do with my frontal lobes. The creative part of my brain was ablaze and working overtime, but I would never be good at counting and reading. I finally got over my lifetime sense of inadequacy when I heard Queen Elizabeth's granddaughter Princess Beatrice describe her own learning disability condition. She could have been describing me. For the first time, I truly understood what my problem was, and I immediately felt better about myself.

There is a Buddhist expression, "turning your poison into medicine." That's the best way to describe what happened to the Flagg Grove School, the scene of my many humiliations at the blackboard. The Harvard historian Henry Louis Gates, Jr. researched my ancestry for his PBS program on genealogy and discovered that my great-grandfather, Benjamin Flagg, was the original owner of the property that was the site for the school. He sold the land for less than market value so the school could be built and Black children would have a place to go for an education. I was profoundly moved by that revelation.

Then, a few years ago, I was approached by the West Tennessee Delta Heritage Center. They proposed moving the old schoolhouse, which by then had become a barn, from Nutbush to nearby Brownsville and turn it into a Tina Turner Museum. We raised enough money to transport the building to the new site, where it was painstakingly restored to show people what it was like to attend an African American school in the South in the 1940's. And it was outfitted with Tina Turner memorabilia to celebrate my career. The windows were designed to appear as they are reflecting a cottonfield. The museum opened in 2104, with my costumes and gold records beside my schoolgirl wooden desk, and would you believe it, an authentic chalkboard just like the one that terrified me when I was a child. It doesn't scare me anymore. Now I'd like to believe it inspires people to overcome whatever obstacles they may experience in life, turning their poison into medicine.

Barbara Walters

Barbara Walters

Audition
By Barbara Walters
Alfred A. Knopf, 2008

Interviewing Celebrities is
More Difficult than Interviewing Presidents

*I*nterviewing celebrities is often harder and much more time-consuming than interviewing newsmakers or world leaders. People seem to think I just pick up the phone and get through to say, Clint Eastwood or Madonna. Not so, over the years there have been endless back-and-forth with agents, public relations representatives, attorneys and managers to secure celebrity interviews. Sometimes it takes months, and in several instances, like Princess Diana or Greta Garbo, years to confirm.

One of the most elusive stars was, you won't be surprised Katharine Hepburn. After pursing her for years we finally settled on a Tuesday in October for our conversation. And wouldn't you know it, the weekend before our meeting, I received an invitation from the League of Women Voters to serve on the questioners' panel that same night for the presidential debate between Jimmy Carter and Ronald Reagan. I phoned Miss Hepburn at her home in Connecticut and asked if she wouldn't mind changing our appointment from that Tuesday to Thursday. She expressed anger saying she already made plans to be in New York City on Tuesday and wasn't of a mind to alter the date because her pet poodle had a veterinarian appointment on Thursday. I subsequently learned from her after we finally did reschedule ten months later that this was a lie and that she was relieved to get out of the interview. I brought her a box of chocolates as a gift. Each time I met her for an interview thereafter, a total of three more times, the first thing she asked is if I had brought any more chocolates with me.

Raquel Welch

Raquel Welch

Raquel: Beyond the Cleavage
By Raquel Welch
Weinstein Books, 2010

The Booby Trap

My first starring role was to be in a dinosaur epic for 20th Century Fox called *One Million Years B.C.* The studio head Dick Zanuck called to tell me that I would be playing the part of Loana in this remake of the 1940 caveman classic. Although I thanked him for my so called big break, all I could think was, "A dinosaur movie? You've got to be kidding me!" But being a single mom with two toddlers to feed and clothe, I thanked him for the opportunity. Privately I figured my performance would disappear without a trace. And it probably would have but for that famous movie poster of me atop a volcano and only in a deerskin bikini.On the first day of shooting, I went straight up to the director and said quite seriously, "Listen Don, I've been studying the script and I was thinking…" He turned to me in amazement and said matter–of–factly, "You we're thinking? Don't." Then he said, "See that rock over there?" I was all ears and eager to learn. "That's Rock A. When I call action, you start running all the way over to Rock B, over there. When you get midway between the two, pretend you see a giant killer turtle coming over that hill. You scream… and we break for lunch. Got it?" I got it all right. A giant killer turtle? But I had no credentials as an actress outside that one laughable line of dialogue: "Me Loana… you Tumak." I felt like I stumbled into a booby-trap; pun intended.

Four brief months later came the release of the infamous movie poster. Several million copies of that image of me were circulated around the world to herald the launch of the film. In the photograph I look so convincing. So formidable standing their astride the rocky landscape in that partially shredded animal skin. I seem alert and slightly defiant, as though ready to defend myself against any caveman who might attempt to tear it off me. The feminist and cultural critic Camille Paglia later described it as, "The indelible image of a woman as queen of nature. She was a lioness: fierce, passionate, and dangerously physical." Anyway, the doeskin bikini struck a chord. Overnight I became every male's fantasy. In one way the image was very apt because I knew I was going to have to fight to stay afloat in the most treacherous of waters: the role of sex symbol at the height of the sexual revolution of the swinging 60's and 70's.

There I was, stranded and easy prey in that desolate frightening realm of overnight success. With the release of that silly poster, in one fell swoop, everything in my life changed and everything about the real me was swept away. The irony of it all is that even though people thought of me as a beauty with a body, in reality I was the mother of two children. Can anybody imagine the girl in that skimpy loincloth with a baby in one arm and pushing a stroller with the other? Kind of destroys the fantasy, doesn't it? But I felt duty-bound and destined to do a cavegirl Loana. She and I get along just fine now. After all, we're basically different sides of the same personality. An if I ask her nicely, she steps aside and gets out of my way. The loincloth is presumably somewhere in mothballs now. When I look back at that poster today, I don't say "Who is she?" Rather, I smile and fondly say, "Oh yeah, I remember you."

Serena Williams

Serena Williams

On the Line
By Serena Williams with Daniel Paisner
Grand Central Publishing, 2009

Playing Against Venus

*O*ver the years, my matches with my older sister Venus have become legendary in tennis circles. People say it's been an epic battle, I don't know about that, but I do know it has put a certain stamp on my career. And on Venus's too. I think. We've been pretty competitive. At one point, going into the 2008 U.S. Open, we were dead even on tour match-ups at eight wins a piece. But we've each had our momentum streaks. Over all these years and in dozens of tournaments, we've been upand down and all over the place.

Throughout my development, there was always Venus to set the standard. At times, when I was little, it seemed like an impossible standard but it was always there. Venus was always the embodiment of my best self. She was both the person and player I hoped to become.During the 2012 U.S. open a reporter asked me an interesting question. She had been looking over my history with Venus in all those Grand Slam tournaments, and she added how many more majors I might have won if Venus had not loomed in my path to on so many occasions. It was a reasonable inquiry. Up to that point I'm guessing Venus had knocked me out of a major on five different occasions, twice in the finals, so just by going by the numbers, I could see where the reporter was heading. But I went a different way in my response. Without hesitating I said, "I don't think I would have won nearly as many."

That wasn't what this reporter expected to hear so I talked about how growing up in U.S. shadow has been such a motivator for me. And how the high standard she set for herself both on and off the court was such a powerful influence on me. How she pushed me to be the best I could be.It's like I like I had all this experience – Venus's experience. Without Venus to lead the way, it would have taken me longer to get where I wanted to be. And then, once I started achieving success on my own, I still looked to Venus as a mode. If she won a major, it fired me up to win the next one. If she went out early to practice after a late night, even after a big win, I went out early too.

Venus beat me many times in tournament finals – so right there – those would have been more titles for me. But I don't see it that way. The way I see it is, who knows if I would have been in those finals without Venus in the first place? It's the difference between a road block and an open lane – and that's all the difference in the world!

Ann & Nancy Wilson

Heart

Ann & Nancy Wilson

Kicking and Screaming:
A Story of Heart, Soul and Rock & Roll
By Ann & Nancy Wilson
It Books, 2012

Women in Rock

*I*n the four decades that my sister Ann and I have been in music, we've been asked countess times what it's like to be "a woman in rock." This question is asked in virtually every interview we do, by men and by women. We sit politely and try to come up with an answer we hope will encourages others. But what I really want to do is scream questions in reply, like "What's it like to be a human being in rock?" What's it like to be a human being on the planet earth?" But looking back, the ninth day of February 1964, a lightning bolt came out of the heavens and struck us. We had our lives before February 9th and we had our lives after. Who we were, and more importantly, who we imagined we could be, shifted forever on that day; we never turned back.

The cause of our transformation was our encounter with four young lads: John, Paul, George and Ringo that Sunday night on TV Ed Sullivan show. "I Want to Hold Your Hand" had become a big radio hit only two weeks before and even in our Marine base elementary school, kids were talking about that song. Their songs, their outfits, their haircuts, every word they uttered and every word they song became imprinted on our brains. We know nothing about love at that point, but we could none the less feel their sexuality literally bursting at the seam. Though those songs now seem so innocent then they felt culturally different, as if the Beatles were purposely pushing hard against the morality of their times. With their hair growing over their ears, to we girls accustomed to the crewcuts of the Marines, that made them seem the most dangerous rebels we had ever seen, even more dangerous than the Sharks and Jets from *West Side Story* by which we previously measured male cooldom. The love we had for the Beatles were far more than a schoolgirl crush. We didn't just fall in love with them; we fell in love with Great Britain, Liverpool, rock and roll, and especially ourselves in a way. They became the lens through which we imagined a bigger world. Similar crushes were happening all over the base, all over America, indeed all over the world. It was like a virus among teen girls. But we soon noticed a chasm between us and other girl Beatle fans. It revealed more about our individual character – who we were and what we would become – than any other facet of our adolescence. We didn't want to become Beatle girlfriends. We wanted to become Beatles. And even though we didn't immediately see ourselves as musicians and rock and rollers – that would come soon enough. It was the music and not Paul's dimples that inspired us. In our house, where we sang and pretended to be Beatles in performances to our parents and their guest, we felt safe imagination was allowed and we felt accepted and loved. We could be female Beatles, and no one would tell us it was absurd. Little did we know that these girlish fun times would lay the foundation for Heart.

Maybe that's why in forty years we've never came up with the perfect answer to the "women in rock" questions. We have no answer for the simple reason that we never thought gender was a barrier to picking up guitars. We started playing rock because we loved music. If we would have known how difficult it would be to be women fronting a band, it might have made us think twice or three times. But probable we would have done it anyway.

Shelly Winters

Shelly Winters

Shelly: Also Known as Shirley
By Shelly Winters
William Morrow and Co., 1980

When Marilyn Monroe and I Were Roommates

Marilyn Monroe and I shared an apartment in Hollywood beginning in 1953, just as she was starting to get lots of publicity. We had a great time furnishing it. The apartment was very nice, though it was a third floor walk-up. It overlooked a little park and had a nice view of the city from a balcony. The only piece of furniture Marilyn owned was a white baby grand piano her mother had left her. "What the hell," I said, "let's look at it. I've acquired a bit of furniture and all you'll need to buy is a bed and dressing table. We'll go to the secondhand shops on Western Avenue and get whatever else we need." Marilyn's face lit up like a kid who had just learned that Santa Claus was real.

The apartment was very nice and was only $227 a month, rent-controlled, but I had to slip the manager $300 to get it. He was a little doubtful about giving this choice apartment to two blondes actresses, so my father came over and happily signed and guaranteed the lease.

One Sunday morning, after we had finally gotten all our secondhand furniture and the place looked all fixed up and real cute, we were playing our records and looking at our photographs in the Academy Players' Directory, the book in which film stars must list their current credits and their agents' names so that producers can contact them. I looked at the photos of all the single leading men and said, "Why must we always put ourselves through this agony we call love?" Marilyn, who was also recovering from an unhappy love affair said, "Wouldn't it be nice if we could be like men and just earn notches on our belts and sleep with the most attractive men and not get emotionally involved?"

Then she came up with an idea. "Let's get a pencil and paper and go through the Directory and make lists of we we'd like to sleep with. But should we just stick to actors and directors?"

"No," I replied. Any man in politics, music, science or literature who appeals to us can be put on our list. Okay? Let's make a game out of it."

"She thought it over. "But aren't most of the good ones dead. I mean the ones in literature and music?"

"Of course not. There's Earnest Hemingway, Irwin Shaw, Clifford Odets, Thornton Wilder."

"He's an actor isn't he?"

"No," I answered, not being too sure. "I believe he's a famous writer like

Eugene O'Neill. But let's also include men like presidents, generals, explorers, industrialists, even animal trainers!"

We decided to take an hour and not show each other our lists until we finished; then we would exchange them. My list contained the names of mostly handsome actors I had fantasized about when I was a teenager, men like Clark Gable, Laurence Oliver, John Garfield, James Mason, Cary Grant, and others. I also included newsmen Chet Huntley and Eric Sevaried, and Ambassador Ralph Bunche and humanitarian Albert Schweitzer for dignity.

When I read Marilyn's choices I dropped the huge Directory in astonishment. She listed names like Charles Laughton, Zero Mostel, Eli Wallach, Charles Boyer, Jean Renoir, Yves Montand and Charles Bickford (who I had heard was not into women); directors John Houston, Elia Kazan and Nicholas Ray; acting coach Lee Strasberg; and Harry Belafonte. Ironically, she listed playwright Arthur Miller who she would later marry but at that time she had never met him. And perhaps out of my same need for dignity, she listed Albert Einstein.

"Marilyn, there is no way you are going to sleep with Einstein. He's the most famous scientist in the world, and besides he an old man."

"That has nothing to do with it," she answered. "I can try, can't I? Those are the rules. Besides, I hear he's very healthy."

Looking back, I don't know how many of her choices she achieved other than her third husband Arthur Miller, but after her tragic death, her personal possessions were bequeathed to Lee Strasberg. When I visited him at his New York City apartment, there on Marilyn's mother's baby grand piano was a large framed photograph of Einstein. On it was written,

"To Marilyn, with respect and love and thanks, Albert Einstein."

Malala Yousafzai

Malala Yousafzai

***I Am Malala: The Story of the Girl Who Stood Up
for Education and Was Shot by the Taliban***
By Malala Yousafzai and Christina Lamb
Little Brown and Company, 2013

Our Descent into Madness

I remember when the Taliban came to our valley. It began a swift, frightening, dangerous and tragic period for my country and our people. But it was even worse because we also became afflicted with a madness of the heart and mind. Let me recall an example.

In Pakistan we have something called the Blasphemy Law, which protects the Holy Quran from desecration. Under former military dictator General Zia's Islamization campaign, the law was made much stricter so that anyone who 'defiles the sacred name of the Holy Prophet can be punished by death or life imprisonment. One day in November 2010 there was a news report about a Christian woman called Asia Bibi who had been sentenced to death by hanging. She was a poor mother of five who picked fruit for a living in a village in Punjab. One hot day she had fetched water for her fellow workers but some of them refused to drink it, saying that the water was 'unclean' because she was a Christian.

They believed that as Muslims they would be defiled by drinking with her. One of them was her neighbor, who was angry because she said Asia Bibi's goat had damaged her water trough. They had ended up in an argument, and of course just as in our arguments at school there were different versions of who said what. One version was that they tried to persuade Asia Bibi to convert to Islam. She replied that Christ had died on the cross for the sins of Christians and asked what the Prophet Mohammad had done for Muslims. One of the fruit pickers reported her to the local imam, who informed the police. She spent more than a year in jail before the case went to court and she was sentenced to death. Since former president Musharraf had allowed satellite television, we now had lots of channels. Suddenly we could witness these events on television. There was outrage round the world and all the talk shows covered the case.

One of the few people who spoke out for Asia Bibi in Pakistan was the governor of Punjab, Salman Taseer. He himself had been a political prisoner as well as a close ally of Benazir. Later on he became a wealthy media mogul. He went to visit Asia Bibi in jail and said that President Ali Zardari should pardon her. He called the Blasphemy Law a 'black law', a phrase which was repeated by some of our TV anchors to stir things up. Then some imams at Friday prayers in the largest mosque in Rawalpindi condemned the governor. A couple of days later, on 4 January 2011, Salman Taseer was gunned down by one of his own bodyguards after lunch in an area of fashionable coffee bars in Islamabad. The man shot him twenty-six times. He later said that he had done it for God after hearing the Friday prayers in his mosque. We were shocked by how many people praised the killer. When he appeared in court even lawyers showered him with rose petals. Meanwhile the imam at the late governor's mosque refused to perform his funeral prayers and the president did not attend his funeral. Our country was going crazy. How was it possible that we were now showering flowers on murderers?

About J. Ajlouny

J. Ajlouny is an author, journalist, editor, and playwright residing in Detroit. When he is not writing, he is reading or engaged in research on any number of topics that satisfy his need for stimulation or escape. When these all fail, he can be found at theaters, museums, and concert halls, soaking up the art that is too often under-appreciated. Hey, somebody has to do it!

Fresh Ink Group

Independent Publisher

❧

Hardcovers
Softcovers
All Ebook Platforms
Worldwide Distribution

❧

Indie Author Services
Book Development, Editing, Proofing
Graphic/Cover Design
Video/Trailer Production
Website Creation
Social Media Management
Writing Contests
Writers' Blogs
Podcasts

❧

Authors
Editors
Artists
Experts
Professionals

❧

FreshInkGroup.com
Email: info@FreshInkGroup.com
Twitter: @FreshInkGroup
Facebook.com/FreshInkGroup
LinkedIn: Fresh Ink Group

Fresh Ink Group

Ajlouny's Word Books

Who Said That?

The Stories Behind Familiar Expressions

For Readers, Writers, Word Lovers, and Trivia Buffs, Fresh Ink Group Explains Whence Come Those Phrases that Color Everyday Speech

J. Ajlouny
Author of *Figuratively Speaking*

Figuratively Speaking

Thesaurus of Expressions & Phrases

Fresh Ink Group's Collection of 7,500+ Figures of Speech, Catchphrases, Idioms, and Colloquialisms Sorted by Meaning & Context

J. Ajlouny
Author of *Who Said That?*

PUSH PULL PRESS
Fresh Ink Group
FreshInkGroup.com

In this boisterous but sensitive drama, playwright J. Ajlouny looks beyond public image to find the heart of this young woman thrust wildly into fame as a sex symbol. Presented as a play-in-the-making within a play, *Marilyn, Norma Jean and Me* weaves biography with humor to explore the movie star's widely speculated plan to leave Hollywood for Broadway. The author imagines her innocence and vulnerability, her friendliness and loyalty, even as the public image threatens to steal her humanity. This play is a must-see or -read for fans of film and stage, not just because it is so good, but for its powerful way of finding the real Norma Jean in the legend known as Marilyn Monroe.

Marilyn, Norma Jean and Me

A dramatization of the movie star's secret plan to leave Hollywood for Broadway

J. Ajlouny

PUSH PULL PRESS

Fresh Ink Group
FreshInkGroup.com

Adventures in Leninland

An Intrepid Journalist's Quest
to Understand a Place
Once Called "The Soviet Union"

J. Ajlouny

The Red Poppy
Josef Stalin at Home

A Dramatization of
Yuri Krotkov's *The Red Monarch*

J. Ajlouny

True Russian Adventures

PUSH PULL PRESS

Fresh Ink Group
FreshInkGroup.com

Adapted Russian Play

Ajlouny's Bard Plays

The Trial of William Shakespeare

A dramatization of the authorship controversy in which the audience renders a verdict

J. Ajlouny

Meet William Shakespeare

A superbly entertaining one-person play starring The Bard himself

J. Ajlouny

PUSH PULL PRESS

Fresh Ink Group
FreshInkGroup.com

COUNTRY MUSIC HALL OF FAME DRUMMER
MARK HERNDON

The
HIGHROAD
Memories from a long trip

What drives a man to spend 26 years performing night after night? To persevere through a stifling tour bus, bad food, strange women, flared tempers, a plane nearly blown from the sky? Just how did that troubled military brat with a dream claw his way from dirt-floor dive-bar shows to the world's biggest stages?

Aviator, author, and Country Music Hall of Fame drummer Mark Herndon lived that dream with one of the most popular and celebrated bands of all time. He learned some hard lessons about people and life, the music industry, the accolades and awards, how easy it is to lose it all . . . and how hard it is to survive, to embrace sobriety, to live even one more day.

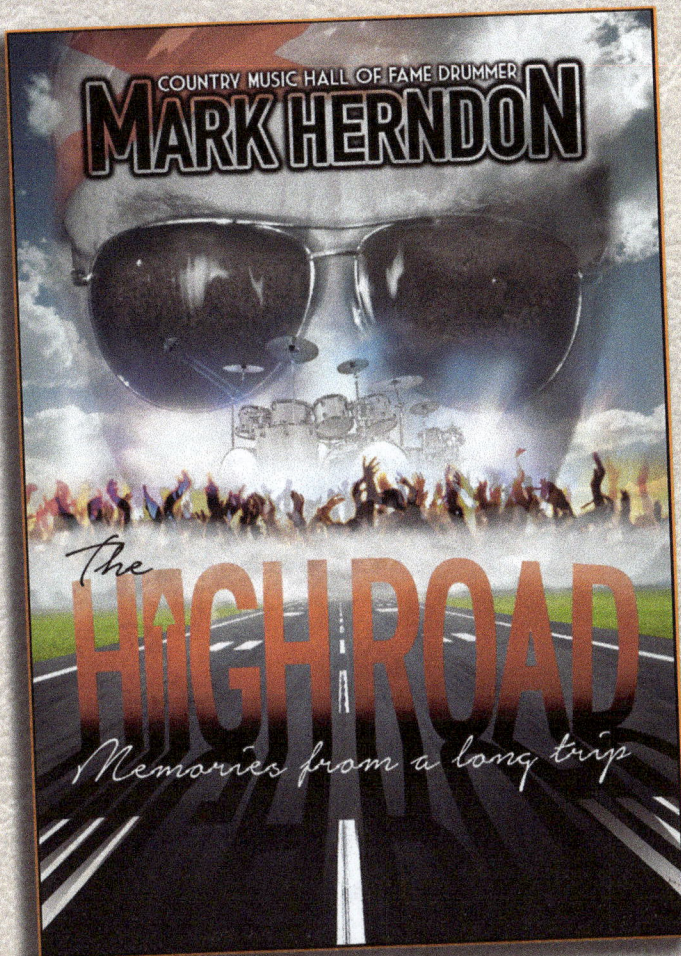

Herndon's poignant memoir offers a tale at once cautionary and inspirational, delightful and heartbreaking, funny yet deeply personal. From innocence to rebellion to acceptance, can a man still flourish when the spotlight dims? Are true forgiveness, redemption, and serenity even possible when the powerful say everything you achieved somehow doesn't even count? That you're not who you and everyone who matters thought you were? Mark Herndon refuses to slow down. So look back, look ahead, and join him on the trip.

He's taking *The High Road.*

Fresh Ink Group
FreshInkGroup.com

Compelling Short Fiction

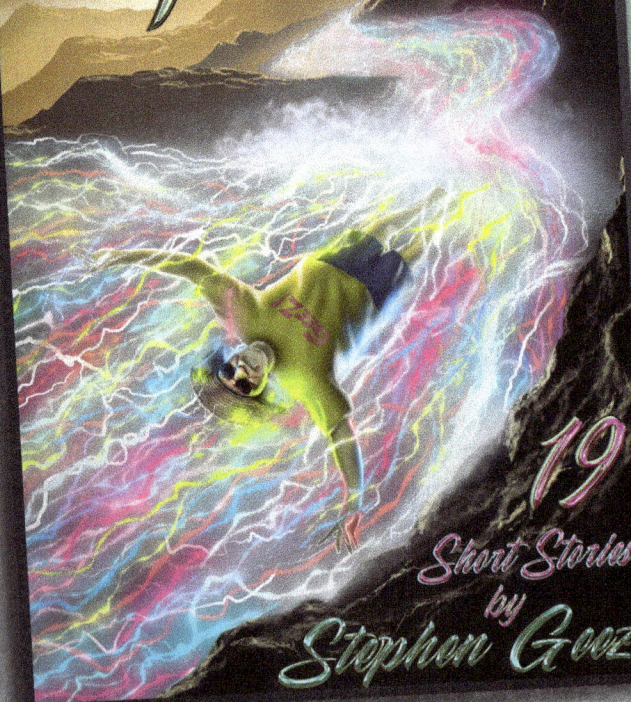

Comes this Time to Float

19 Short Stories by Stephen Geez

STRANGE HWY

Short Stories

Beem Weeks

Fresh Ink Group
FreshInkGroup.com

HELLO, CHATTANOOGA!

Famous People
Who Have Visited the Tennessee Valley

David Carroll

VOLUNTEER BAMA DAWG

A TV Guy's Love
Letter to the South

David Carroll
Author of *Chattanooga Radio and Television*

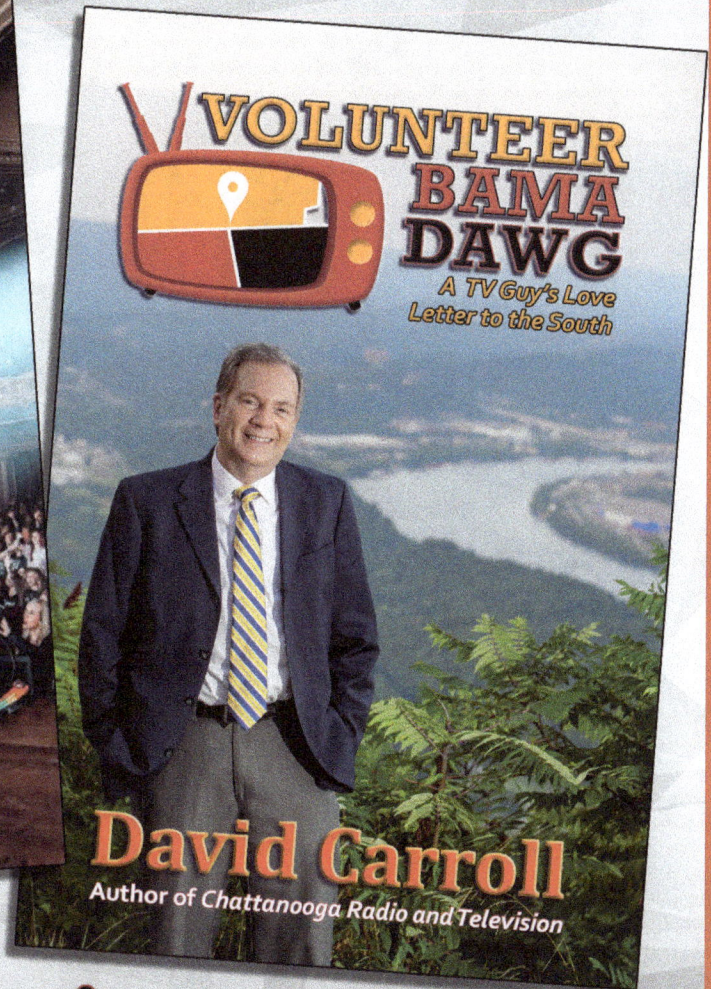

Chattanooga's Voice of the South!

www.ingramcontent.com/pod-product-compliance
Lightning Source LLC
Chambersburg PA
CBHW050918150426
42812CB00050B/1728